CREATING AN

excellent salon

BUSINESS PRACTICE FOR BEAUTY THERAPISTS

Iris Rigazzi-Tarling

Hodder & Stoughton

A MEMBER OF THE HODDER HEADLINE GROUP

Dedication

For my mother, Mary

Acknowledgements

I wish to thank my colleagues in Beauty Therapy for their suggestions for the content of this book and in particular Frances Hilder of Kingston College of Further Education who read the manuscript.

I would like to thank the interviewees for their valuable contribution, Sheila Lewis for her specialist advice on the accountancy section and John Cragg, Director of IPTI, for his assistance with the latest NVQ information.

Finally, my grateful thanks to my dear friend, Doris Bunce, who typed the manuscript.

The author and publishers would like to thank the following for permission to reproduce photographs in this book:

Front cover: Nemectron GmbH; Ultratone Ltd; Gibbon Bridge Country House Hotel
Back cover: Natural Woman Health and Beauty Clinic
Inside photographs: Taylor Reeson Laboratories, pp 90, 91, 92, 102; George Solly Organisation Ltd, p 91; Natural Woman Health and Beauty Clinic, pp 121, 125; Ellisons, p 91, 97; Susan Molyneux, pp 99; Thomson Directories, p. 108.

British Library Cataloguing in Publication Data

Rigazzi-Tarling, Iris
    Creating an Excellent Salon: Business
    Practice for Beauty Therapists
    I. Title
    646.7068

ISBN 0 340 58308 8

First published 1994
Impression number   10 9 8 7 6 5 4 3 2 1
Year   1998 1997 1996 1995 1994

Typeset by Wearset, Boldon, Tyne & Wear.
Printed in Great Britain for Hodder & Stoughton Educational, a division of Hodder Headline Plc, Mill Road, Dunton Green, Sevenoaks, Kent TN13 2YA by Thomson Litho Ltd.

Contents

Preface

Creating an Excellent Salon is intended for students taking courses in beauty therapy and management. It's structure is simple and concise, and the main skill development areas are:

- personal and inter-personal skills;
- supervisory skills;
- the business person/employer/owner/trainer/counsellor; and
- financial and business management and development.

The contents include syllabus criteria of major awarding bodies:
- City and Guilds Certificate in Beauty Therapy;
- BTEC – National and Higher National Certificates;
- SCOTVEC – Higher National Certificate and Higher National Diploma;
- International Therapy Examination Council;
- International Health and Beauty Council;
- Confederation of International Beauty Therapy and Cosmetology;
- International Aestheticiennes;

and is designed to meet components for NVQs (National Vocational Qualifications) and SVQs (Scottish Vocational Qualifications) levels 1, 2, 3, 4.

Much of the material in this book could be relevant to other courses leading to GNVQs and GSVQs (General National Vocational Qualifications).

The book is designed to be a source of information. Addresses will appear in the text and are also listed at the back of the book.

Most countries offering courses leading to international qualifications in beauty therapy have laws that are similar to those in Britain in relation to acquiring a business licence, the environment and the payment of taxes. The overseas reader is therefore encouraged to seek all the relevant information as suggested in the book, but in relation to the country in which she/ he is living. This is important because legislation in the USA, Australia and South Africa is different from state to state.

Introduction

Have you got what it takes? So often one hears this question being put to prospective employees. This book is designed to show you what it takes – the rest is up to you!

The beauty industry demands a variety of skills and a very high standard of professional expertise if you are to be successful. This book aims to present simply the key areas that will help you to develop yourself and your expertise in the progression from:

assistant → manager → salon owner

PART I

Know yourself and your profession

CHAPTER 1 *Know yourself*

OBJECTIVES

Knowing yourself will help you to make correct choices concerning your work and your future. Self-evaluation, knowing your strengths and weaknesses, and identifying your needs, personality type and values will help you to see yourself as the character you really are and to project yourself as the person you want to be and help you to be successful.

Life is constantly changing and so you will need to adjust and change. In order to achieve your aims, set short-term targets to be realistic and to mark your achievement. You will need to evaluate your performance on a regular basis if you really want to know yourself, and be successful.

It is vital if you are going to operate a successful business that you first know yourself. When you are able to evaluate yourself and know your strengths and weaknesses, you will be able to identify your needs and discern strengths and weaknesses in your colleagues. There are certain key areas:

Identify

your strengths and weaknesses	your character type	your values	your aims

These will help you to:

KNOW YOURSELF AND PLAN YOUR FUTURE.

Strengths and weaknesses

What type of person are you? Are you:

honest	enthusiastic
smart	friendly
willing	self-reliant
ambitious	patient
hard-working	sympathetic
self-confident	energetic
strong	competent

Character type

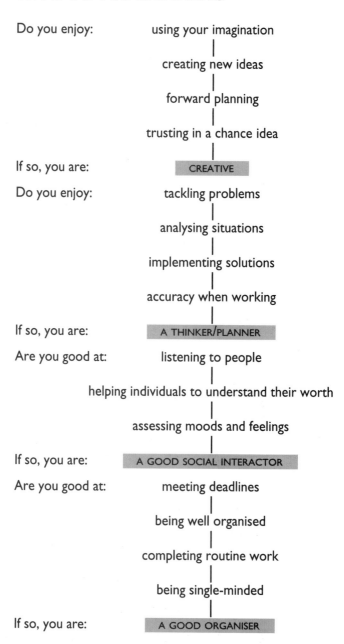

WHAT DO YOU LIKE DOING

Do you enjoy: using your imagination

creating new ideas

forward planning

trusting in a chance idea

If so, you are: CREATIVE

Do you enjoy: tackling problems

analysing situations

implementing solutions

accuracy when working

If so, you are: A THINKER/PLANNER

Are you good at: listening to people

helping individuals to understand their worth

assessing moods and feelings

If so, you are: A GOOD SOCIAL INTERACTOR

Are you good at: meeting deadlines

being well organised

completing routine work

being single-minded

If so, you are: A GOOD ORGANISER

Fortunately, as we are all individuals we do not fit into one 'box-type'. We often find we have more than one major quality. This is when a knowledge of our own values can assist us.

Values

Analysing your values and adding them to your natural strengths and aptitudes helps you to begin a happy and successful career. Once you have decided on your own goals, you aim for them.

Do you value:

A SECURE WORKING ENVIRONMENT?

If so, look for a position with a regular routine, closely defined duties and a regular wage and benefits.

Do you value:

FREEDOM AND FLEXIBILITY?

Would you like your working environment to be casual and relaxed with shifts or flexitime? Would you value being able to use your own initiative?

Do you value:

ACHIEVEMENT?

If so you must set your aims at short-term goals, and you must work in a situation where your achievement is recognised and rewarded.

Do you value:

FINANCIAL SUCCESS?

If you aim to achieve a good income, you must be prepared to go for high salaries and lots of perks. You must have plenty of skills and be competent and determined.

Do you value:

POWER AND LEADERSHIP?

If you want power and leadership – to be the best and to arrive at the top – you must look for a working environment that gives you plenty of experience and opportunities to succeed.

Do you value:

PEOPLE?

Working closely with colleagues and having time to talk to clients can make your working life a pleasure. Good communication skills and a friendly working environment are sometimes lost in the busy, non-stop pressure of a high-powered business. You must decide on the 'right' work-place.

Aims

Once you have identified your aptitudes and values, you are able to identify your aims and set goals.

 Short-term targets are best if you are to be successful. Your aims will also be governed by the type of image you intend to project.

 Will you be a confident, smart, knowledgeable, reliable optimist?

 Will you build your reputation on your skills and personal qualities? What will *you* do?

SELF - ASSESSMENT EVALUATION

1   WHAT TYPE OF PERSON ARE YOU?

List your *personal* qualities.

2   IDENTIFY YOUR CHARACTER TYPE(S).

(a) Are you an organiser or a thinker?
Are you a creative person?
Are you a social interactor?
Answer:

(b) Make a list of your strengths and weaknesses.

3   WHAT ARE YOUR VALUES?

(a) Do you value security?
(b) Do you value freedom and flexibility?

(c) Do you value financial success?
(d) Do you value power and leadership?
(e) Do you value achievement?
(f) Do you value people?
    Place these in order of importance to you.

4   YOUR AIMS.

How will you decide on your aims?
Answer:

5 Why is it important to 'know yourself'?
Answer:

When you have completed this section you will have successfully made your first evaluation.

CHAPTER 2   *Know Your Profession*

O BJECTIVES

This chapter explains the importance of holding recognised qualifications in beauty therapy and in being a professional. The major associations set the standards for the professionals. Professional standards start with your personal standards. These can never be too high. When qualified, membership of an association will give you status and professional 'back up'. Finally, when you apply for a position you will need to prepare a CV. This is your passport into work and needs regular updating as you progress in your career.

Recognised qualifications

If you want to be successful in your work you must:

- know your trade or profession; and
- be professional.

You must hold qualifications that are recognised in this country, and if you intend to work abroad, your qualifications must have international status. Recognised qualifications mean that **you**:

 have followed a professional training of a specified length

have learnt the practical and theoretical skills demanded for your chosen career in beauty therapy.

Major awarding bodies

Most technical/state colleges and private schools take the examinations of one or more of the major awarding bodies. Major examining boards offer similar qualifications and most of these are of international status or are recognised by international associations for membership.

NATIONAL AWARDING BODIES:

- *C & G* (City and Guilds of London Institute)
C & G was founded in 1878 and it offers nationally accepted qualifications. There is a one- or two-year course for the Beauty Therapy Certificate. The course may be part-time or full-time. It is available through technical/further education colleges throughout the UK and Eire.

- *BTEC*
BTEC approves work-related programmes of study organised by colleges and polytechnics in England and Wales. BTEC offers a two-year, full-time course for the National Diploma in Beauty Therapy, and when this diploma has been gained, a student may study for the Higher National Diploma (HND).

SCOTVEC
SCOTTISH VOCATIONAL
EDUCATION COUNCIL

- *SCOTVEC*
SCOTVEC is responsible for developing, awarding and accrediting vocational qualifications, including Scottish Vocational Qualifications (SQVs) in Scotland (NVQs in England and Wales), SCOTVEC's beauty therapy qualifications are HNC (Higher National Certificate) and HND.

INTERNATIONAL AWARDING BODIES:

 INTERNATIONAL
THERAPY
EXAMINATION
COUNCIL
LIMITED

- *ITEC* (The International Therapy Examination Council)
ITEC was formed in 1973. ITEC courses operate in colleges and private schools throughout the world. The Aestheticienne and Psychiatrics Diplomas can be gained in one year. On completion the honours diploma may be taken if a satisfactory passmark has been obtained.

- *CIBTAC* (The Confederation of International Beauty Therapy and Cosmetology)
CIBTAC offers an Aestheticienne Diploma and Body Therapy Diploma which can be completed in one year. Courses operate in colleges and private schools in the UK and abroad.

- *CIDESCO* (Le Comite Internationale d'Esthetiques et de Cosmetologie)
BABTAC organises the examinations for CIDESCO. CIBTAC is the British examining board accepted by CIDESCO for conducting these examinations. The CIDESCO course can be studied if students gain the required pass rate in CIBTAC examinations.

- *IHBC* (International Health and Beauty Council)
Started in 1962, IHBC courses operate in colleges and private

beauty schools in the UK and abroad. IHBC offers the International Beauty Therapist's Diploma, which can be completed in one year, and also the International Master's Diploma in Health and Beauty Therapy.

- *IA* (International Aestheticiennes)
  Started in the 1980s, IA examines students in an in-salon situation, placing more attention on practical ability. A diploma can be gained in beauty therapy.

- *NVQs* (National Vocational Qualifications)
  In 1986 the National Council for Vocational Qualifications (NCVQ) was established to reform the National System of Vocational Qualifications. The NCVQ is not an examining body, but it will give its seal of approval to qualifications if they meet its criteria. The qualification is then identified as an NVQ, and will bear the NCVQ's logo.

  The NCVQ has set *four* levels of awards, and each level relates to a range of skills, knowledge and understanding to apply these in employment. The benefits of NVQs are:

  nationally recognised by employers
  |
  qualifications within a system that is accessible to everyone
  |
  qualifications that provide equal opportunities for all who achieve national standards of performance
  |
  qualifications that fit into a simple framework
  |
  qualifications that are based on competence and that are recognised no matter how they are acquired

- *HBTTB* (The Health and Beauty Therapy Training Board)
  This was created in March 1989 to be the industry's lead body for beauty therapy and allied remedial treatments. The Board is establishing the standards required for the industry and setting the competence levels so that major beauty therapy awarding bodies will be able to apply to the NCVQ for accreditation.

NVQs

At the time of writing, NVQs levels 1 and 2 have been agreed by the HBTTB for SCOTVEC, City and Guilds, CIBTAC and IHBC. It is anticipated that level 3 will be agreed in the near future when the remaining awarding bodies will apply for accreditation.

The NVQ levels are generally defined as:

Level 1, Foundation Level, where all work is carried out under direct supervision:

- Assisting with Reception, stock handling and Treatment Services.

Level 2, where the individual is expected to be able to perform routine tasks and simple treatments under their own initiative:

- Marketing and Cosmetic Beauty Services.

Level 3, where the individual is capable of performing a full range of salon treatments and contributes to the management of the establishment:

- Beauty Therapy Corrective Treatments;
- Supervisory skills (in addition to a variety of additional treatments including aromatherapy, epilation, remedial camouflage, sports massage.

Level 4, Management.

Good practical and theoretical skills

In addition to holding a recognised qualification, you will need to be experienced in all your practical and theoretical skills. You will also need to be numerate and demonstrate good written language.

Personal management skills

If you are going to be successful you must learn how to manage yourself, your time and your aims.

Regular evaluation of yourself will ensure that you are on the right track and that you will develop your aims. Manage your time well.

Being a professional

Professionalism and a good personal code of ethics are acquired by following a professional training. The term 'professional' is used often, but what does it mean to the beauty therapist? It means that there are many ways in which she/he must demonstrate her/his professional skills.

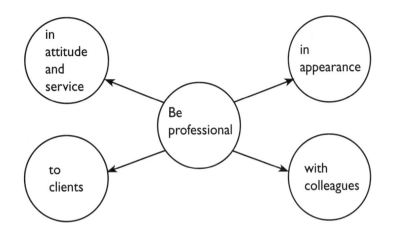

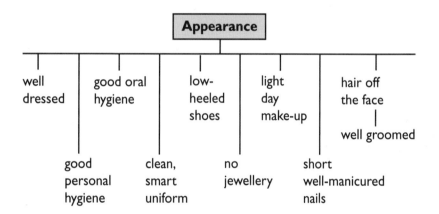

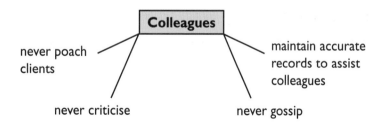

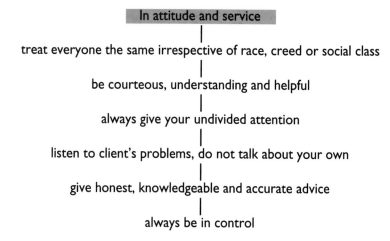

In attitude and service

|

treat everyone the same irrespective of race, creed or social class

|

be courteous, understanding and helpful

|

always give your undivided attention

|

listen to client's problems, do not talk about your own

|

give honest, knowledgeable and accurate advice

|

always be in control

Major professional associations

When adopting a professional approach to work, you are demonstrating the standards of your industry and when qualified you will want to join a professional association.

Most examination awarding bodies are linked to professional international associations, so that once qualified you can identify and belong to a recognised association that has branches throughout the world. Membership to an association gives you the trademark of a professional and a stamp of approval for the public and the industry.

What membership of an association might offer **you**.

a means of identification

|

member's badge and certificate

|

professional indemnity insurance

|

regular newsletter

|

meetings to update your knowledge and meet colleagues

|

an advice service

|

reduced subscriptions to professional journals

|

special rates for private health insurances

|

special rates for AA/RAC membership

All professional associations will have their own code of ethics. They have a worldwide standard to maintain, and members are expected to abide by this code to ensure that the standards of their profession are upheld.

Below is a typical code of ethics of an international association.

Figure 2.1   *IPTI Code of Ethics*

Code of Ethics

The Independent Professional Therapists International, hereinafter referred to as I.P.T.I. or the Association, require that all members without regard to grade, status or position should at all times maintain the highest level of professional conduct.

THE CODE is intended to help establish what is appropriate and acceptable practice and to protect members of the public from improper practices.

THE CODE is also intended to help maintain honourable standards of behaviour of members, towards each other, toward clients and members of the public and toward other professional institutions and their members.

THE CODE is not intended to place restrictions on individual members but does place a member under obligation to his profession and professional body.

1. A member must always act with due regard to the laws, customs and practices of the country in which he or she works.

2. A member shall practice only within the limits of his professional training and competency.

3. A member shall not treat any person who to his knowledge could be suffering from any condition likely to be affected by the treatment without the knowledge and consent of the person's medical practitioner.

4. A member who suspects a client is affected by any condition medical or otherwise beyond the range of his training must decline treatment and advise the client to consult an appropriately qualified practitioner.

5. Membership incurs an obligation to uphold the dignity and honour of the profession, to exalt its standing and to extend its usefulness to the public. The conduct of members shall at all times be both becoming and creditable to the profession.

6. A member should always act professionally towards clients and fellow practitioners, should maintain secrecy and confidentiality in his work and not criticise the work of a fellow practitioner.

7. No member shall for any reason offer treatments, aid or advice to any person known to be under the care of another member of I.P.T.I. without the consent of such member.

8. A member temporarily taking charge of a client of another member shall make no effort to influence such client to leave his usual therapist and shall uphold as far as is consistently possible and shall in no way disparage the methods of any such member. In consultation due regard shall be paid to the therapist in charge of the case.

9. A member who has been employed as an assistant by another member shall not at the termination of his employment or on the decease of his former employer where the practice of his former employer has been purchased by another member circularise or otherwise attempt to induce clients to forsake the practice of such former employer.

10. All duly constituted medical bodies shall be respected and endeavours made to merit the esteem of medical practitioners with whom members may come into contact.

11. The fact of clients changing to another therapist or another setting up in practice near at hand should not be allowed to influence the friendly relationship which should exist among all members.

12. A member may use the appropriate designatory letters on letterheads and in advertisements and publicity providing that the placement and content of such advertising material always conforms to the high standards of professional practice without hint or reference to any form of impropriety.

13. In cases where a member acts jointly with or practices in partnership with one or more persons (whether they are all members of the Association or not) they shall not use the designatory letters of the Association after their joint names or after the title of the firm or in any manner directly or indirectly calculated to lead to the assumption that all such persons are individually all members of the Association.

14. Any member who resigns membership or permits their membership to lapse may not display the Association certificate and must cease all use of the Association's designatory letters, logo and other devices.

TREATMENT OF CLIENTS BY THERAPISTS OF THE OPPOSITE SEX

In some clinics and salons it is necessary and accepted that treatments be given by therapists on clients of the opposite sex. In such situations a strictly professional approach must be adopted. There shall be no unnecessary disrobing of the client and the therapist shall be properly dressed to avoid any provocation. It is desirable that a third person be on hand and that the treatment cubicle be accessible.

DISCIPLINE

All members are subject to the Association's Code of Ethics.
The Association reserves the right to investigate any reported incident of misconduct or breach of the Association's Code of Ethics and to take whatever action it deems to be appropriate in the interest of the Association and the Profession at large.

In enforcing the Code of Ethics and subsidiary ethical rules and in endeavouring to prevent improper practices being performed by persons other than our members we depend on the co-operation of all members. If members learn of breaches of the code or know of establishments permitting activities which reflect upon and lower the status of our profession and bring our work into disrepute then they should report such matters in writing. All such reports will be treated in the strictest confidence.

INDEPENDENT PROFESSIONAL THERAPISTS INTERNATIONAL, 8 ORDSALL ROAD, RETFORD, NOTTS DN22 7PL, ENGLAND

Major associations are:

- *IFHB* (The International Federation of Health and Beauty Therapists)
  IHBC is the examination board associated with IFHB.

- *IPTI* (Independent Professional Therapists International)
  IPTI is an independent association and accepts members who hold recognised qualifications in beauty and therapy.

- *BABTAC* (British Association of Beauty Therapy and Cosmetology)
  CIBTAC is the examination board associated with BABTAC.

Producing a curriculum vitae

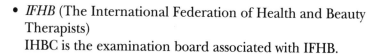

When applying for a position, your employer will want to know:

your educational background
your skills
your work experience

The outline of your educational and professional history is called a *curriculum vitae* (CV) and is presented in a particular way. The sample opposite will help you to create your own CV:

Your completed CV should be typed/word processed for easy reading and good presentation. It should have a clear, concise layout. It is a good idea to produce several copies.

Your CV should be updated regularly so that all your achievements are recorded.

Many employers send a formal application form when you apply for a position. This may record the information in a similar way to your CV. You should complete the application form and return it with a letter of application.

Many beauty therapists choose to make an application for a job even if there is not a position being advertised. This direct approach means that the beauty therapist can think about the type of organisation where she/he would like to work. She/he can send a CV and letter of application to the various companies and ask that the CV is retained on their files for future reference.

This practice is very common and employers like to maintain a recruitment file.

CURRICULUM VITAE

Name:	Anne Other
Date of birth:	07.09.73
Address:	72 Any Road, Anytown, Herts, HRS QSZ
Telephone no:	. . . .
Marital status:	Single
Car driver:	Full licence
School/further education	Peaks Comprehensive Natler Road Anytown September 1984 – July 1991
	Anytown FE College, Anytown September 1991 – July 1992

Examinations:

GCSE	Passes	Grade
English Language		A
English Literature		B
French		B
History		A
Biology		B
Physics		C
Art		B

'A' Level		
English		B

City and Guilds
Certificate in Beauty Therapy
Certificate in Electrolysis

Work experience:	Debenhams Department Store Anytown Two weeks April 1989
Interests/hobbies:	Swimming, reading, drawing, cycling
References:	Mrs R Scott, Head Teacher, Peaks Comprehensive School, Anytown (former head teacher)
	Mr P Maitland, The Manager, Debenhams Department Store, Anytown (former employer)

Figure 2.2 *Sample Curriculum Vitae*

If you want *your* CV to be retained make sure that it is:

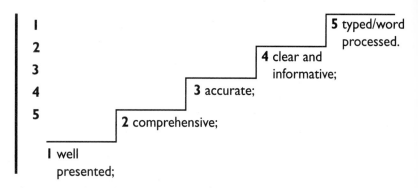

1
2
3
4
5

1 well
  presented;

2 comprehensive;

3 accurate;

4 clear and
  informative;

5 typed/word
  processed.

THINGS TO DO

1 Make a list of at least 12 points that you consider to be important qualities as a professional beauty therapist.

2 What is the difference between City and Guilds and IPTI.

3 Why was the NCVQ established?

4 (a) Write to *two* associations requesting membership details.
  (b) Compare what they offer for membership.

5 Prepare your own CV.

6 (a) Select *three* companies/organisations where you might like to work.
  (b) For each company list *three* reasons why you might like to work within the organisation.

PART 2 *The role of the salon owner/ manager(ess)*

CHAPTER 3 *The organiser*

OBJECTIVES

This chapter explains the importance of good leadership skills for the salon owner. In order to be successful she/he must be assertive, motivated and organised and be able to work well with people. Effective organisation of the staff and the salon is reflected in an efficient service to your clientele.

Good organisational skills

The salon owner should be able to demonstrate good leadership and good organisational skills by establishing and operating a business with an efficient team of staff.

The salon owner will create a general atmosphere of:

where employees can work in a stimulated, friendly environment.

The salon owner will ensure that:

aims and objectives
are clearly defined
|
the employee is able to be
flexible and adjust to change
|
the employee feels secure in
a relatively structured
environment (with a relaxed atmosphere)

Good management/leadership is about employing all the necessary skills so that you can achieve your goals effectively with the support of your staff.

As manager(ess)/leader you must be a *thinker*; you will need many skills and as a person you must identify with your own *character type*:

- A *dynamic* person can be too overpowering for employees.
- A *passive* person can be too laid back!

What sort of manager(ess)/leader you are will depend very much on the skills you will need.
You will need to be:

Organised	→ get the important things done first.
Assertive	→ see your employees' point of view even though you have your own.
Motivated	→ recognise opportunities and be stimulated to act.
A good leader	→ values the employees' contributions; asks their advice and encourages decision-making.
Able to delegate	→ give your employees tasks which they can do (never delegate tasks that you are not prepared to do yourself).
Able to counsel	→ listen to the problems of your staff in private, reassure them and help them to find a solution.
Able to offer praise and encouragement	→ verbal reward for a job well done encourages respect.
Able to evaluate	→ seeing 'all' sides, able to 'stand back' and objectively assess the situation.

The salon owner knows how to manage time efficiently. Good organisational skills are transmitted to staff and clients instantly. The organised person presents:

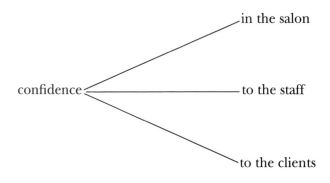

Business is founded on **service.** Reliable, efficient organisation of the salon suggests good **service** and gives staff and clients **confidence** in you.

Figure 3.1 *The organiser pyramid*

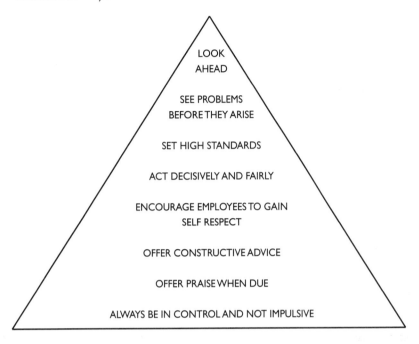

LOOK AHEAD

SEE PROBLEMS BEFORE THEY ARISE

SET HIGH STANDARDS

ACT DECISIVELY AND FAIRLY

ENCOURAGE EMPLOYEES TO GAIN SELF RESPECT

OFFER CONSTRUCTIVE ADVICE

OFFER PRAISE WHEN DUE

ALWAYS BE IN CONTROL AND NOT IMPULSIVE

THINGS TO DO

1 List the leadership qualities you possess.

2 Describe how you would attempt to develop or improve your leadership skills.

3 State two possible situations (for each) that could arise in the salon which would test your skills:

as an employer   an organiser
a leader   a delegator

CHAPTER 4 *Staff selection*

OBJECTIVES

Staff selection requires managerial skills. You will need to be able to prepare a job description/specification and advertisements and interview applicants. You will need to demonstrate good interviewing techniques if you are able to obtain the 'right' staff.

After you have selected and appointed staff, you will need to issue a written statement or contract. There are various contracts that you will need to be familiar with, as well as knowing how to terminate a contract and dismiss staff. Some knowledge of various Acts – Equal Pay Act, the Sexual Discrimination Acts, the Race Relations Act and the Misrepresentation Act – will provide you with a good background knowledge as an employer.

Staff selection is a managerial task. When selecting staff you will want to employ people who are going to help make your business successful. You will want your staff to be able to perform many duties in addition to looking smart and:

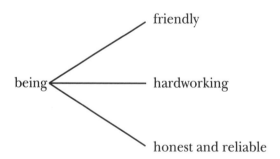

being
- friendly
- hardworking
- honest and reliable

Job specification

First you will prepare a **job description specification** which will outline:

- the job title;
- the employee's immediate superior;
- the duties and responsibilities;

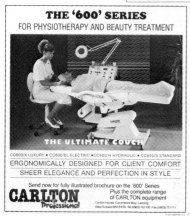

Figure 4.1   *Health and Beauty Salon magazine*

Figure 4.2   *Sample advertisement*

• the experience and qualifications necessary to fill the position (physical and personal skills);
• the pay and package you will offer.

Next, you will place an advertisement in places where you feel will gain the best response. A professional journal such as *Health & Beauty Salon* would be ideal, but you might like to consider your local paper, and employment agencies. An advertisement might look like the one below (remember, you are paying for the size of the advert, so you need to say everything necessary and as briefly as possible).

> *Any Salon*
> Anytown
>
> requires a
> Beauty Therapist
>
> Experience preferred
> International qualifications
>
> Tel: ....

The interview

What to look for

Once you have received applications and CVs you will need to make a list of suitable applicants and then ask them to attend an interview.

Make sure you advise them clearly about the interview:

• the time;
• the place;
• anything they will need to bring, for example, an overall (if you wish to see a demonstration of practical skills).

Interviewing demands a number of skills:

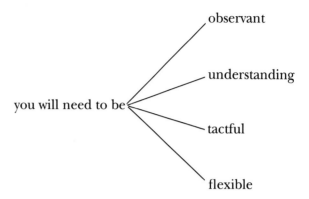

you will need to be
- observant
- understanding
- tactful
- flexible

in order to establish a good rapport.

A good interviewer allows the applicant to talk about her/himself. You will ask *open questions*, that is, questions which do not imply answers. An example of this could be: 'Tell me about your . . .', which allows the interviewee to give detailed answers. If you are too rigid or act impatiently, the interviewee will become tense. You should also be aware of the applicant's non-verbal behaviour. Are the applicant's actions telling you something different to what is being said?

If the applicant is to demonstrate her/his skills or abilities and outline her/his previous experience, a relaxed, friendly atmosphere is necessary. The following points should assist you:

THE INTERVIEWER

should use the CV as a basis for the interview
|
should ask the applicant to expand on certain areas
|
should be led by the applicant's answers
|
should ask open questions
|
should be attentive – and listen to the applicant's replies
|
should check her/his career aims
|
should establish what motivates her/him
|
should allow the applicant to ask questions

THE INTERVIEWEE

should be smartly dressed
|
should be honest
|
should be able to analyse her/his experience and career aims
|
should be knowledgeable about her/his work
|
should be asked questions about her/his skills
|
should ask prepared questions

You may wish to see some applicants a second time before deciding on who to employ. You will need to consider following up references, and should reply as soon as possible to applicants you will not be seeing again.

ALWAYS KEEP YOUR APPLICATIONS ON FILE – YOU MAY WISH TO REFER TO THEM AGAIN IN THE FUTURE.

Contracts of employment

Once you have selected staff, you are required by law to give them written terms and conditions of employment – a written statement of employment – within 13 weeks from the date they commenced working for you. (This is not required if the employee works for less than 16 hours per week, or for long-standing employees who have worked 8 hours a week for at least 5 years.) This is not officially a contract and need not be signed by employer or employee to be enforced.

UNWRITTEN CONTRACTS

'In law, employees have a contract of employment as soon as they start work even when the written statement of its terms and conditions required by the 1978 Act has not been given to the employee.' (PL711) Dept. of Employment.

These exist where no formal contract has been made. If the verbal contract is broken, it is often a difficult procedure to prove it, so a formal contract is advisable.

CONTRACT OF EMPLOYMENT

The contract of employment differs from a statement of employment in that it is usually a **formal agreement** which both the employer and employee sign. Problems can arise with contracts, so it is advisable to have the contract drawn up by a solicitor. The Contracts of Employment Act 1972 and the Employment Protection (Consolidation) Act 1978 states the minimum details must be included in the written statement/ contract:

- name of employer;
- name of employee;
- date employment began;
- any employment with a previous employer which counts as part of the employee's continuous period of employment and, if so, the date at which the period of continuous employment began;
- title of the job;
- hours of work;
- rate of pay including overtime, commission and frequency of payment;
- sick pay (terms);
- holiday pay;
- holiday entitlement;
- pension information or scheme;
- disciplinary and grievance procedures;
- safety rules;
- length of notice for termination of employment.

There are various types of contracts.

OPEN-ENDED CONTRACTS

These are for an unspecified period of time and are terminable by either side giving notice as stated in the contract.

FIXED-TERM CONTRACTS

These are for a certain period of time and will automatically come to an end.

SHORT-TERM CONTRACTS

These are for three months or less. If the employee is offered repeated short-term contracts, this is regarded by law as continuous employment.

TERMINATION OF A CONTRACT

Employment can be terminated by either party giving the correct notice as stated in the contract. This might not necessarily meet the requirements of current legislation. The Employment Protection (Consolidation) Act 1978 states that the employer must give:

one week's notice after four weeks' continuous employment

two weeks' notice after two years

one weeks' notice for each year of continuous employment up to a maximum of twelve weeks.

The employee must give at least:

one week's notice after four weeks' service (unless the contract of employment states otherwise)

the employee's request can be oral or written

the employer must reply within 14 days.

Dismissing staff

When appointing staff, you will no doubt take great care to ensure that you have selected the right people for the position. However, circumstances change and the performance of individual employees may also change. A minor problem, such as lateness, usually shows up on the appraisal form, but if there is no improvement it could be a reason for dismissal.

Misconduct at work and an inability to do the required work are main reasons for dismissal.

According to the main Employment Acts: if dismissal is *fair* there is a certain procedure that must be followed:

there must be sufficient reason **and** the employer must have acted reasonably

The employee who persists in being late to work cannot be dismissed without warning. This would be **unfair**. In order for the situation to be fair, the employer would have warned her/him at least three times:

- an informal verbal warning;
- a formal verbal warning;
- a formal written warning;
- a final written warning.

The employer would be given a suitable period to change and correct the matter. Then the dismissal would be fair if there had been no improvement.

Fair dismissal means:

the reason for dismissal has been identified

|

the reason was fair

|

the employer's action was reasonable

Immediate dismissal would be acceptable for **gross misconduct**, for example, stealing.

It is the employer's responsibility to ensure fair dismissal. If the employee is not satisfied, she/he can take the matter to an industrial tribunal. The tribunal then considers whether the employer has followed a discipline which is acceptable to the specifications of the Advisory Conciliation and Arbitration Service (ACAS).

Figure 4.3
Fair and unfair dismissal booklet PL714
Employee's rights on insolvency of employer booklet PL718

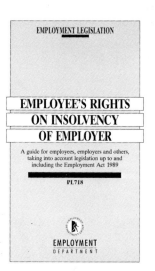

Why people are unemployable

The beauty industry demands high standards, hard work and a high degree of skill competency. People who are unemployable in the beauty industry usually present:

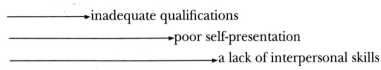

inadequate qualifications

poor self-presentation

a lack of interpersonal skills

Their work references often show that:

performance is poor
|
they are irresponsible
|
they are poor time-keepers
|
they are often unreliable
|
they do not respond to personal counselling

Acts relating to employment

You will need to be familiar with parts of certain Acts relating to employment or your solicitor will advise you.

Equality in the workplace is an important factor and the Equal Pay Act of 1970 and the Sexual Discrimination Acts of 1975 and 1986 are directly concerned with equality. The Equal Pay Act says that employees who do the **same** work:

- must be employed on the **same** pay; *and*
- must be employed on the **same** terms.

The Sexual Discrimination Acts advise that it is an offence to discriminate between married or unmarried women and men.

The Race Relations Act 1976 says that as an employer you cannot discriminate against employees on the grounds of colour, race or nationality.

The person entering into a contract is protected by the Misrepresentation Act 1967. A claim can be made if a person claims misrepresentation of terms and suffers damage.

THINGS TO DO

1 List the personal qualities that you think are essential for a good manager(ess).

2 List the qualities you would look for when interviewing prospective staff.

3 Design a small advertisement for an experienced therapist and find out what it would cost to place it in a local paper and a professional journal.

4 Prepare a job description for an experienced beauty therapist in a large salon.

5 Make a list of questions you would ask an applicant at an interview.

6 Briefly describe the importance of a written contract of employment;
   (a) for a new member of staff; and
   (b) for the beauty therapist who is leaving.

7 Write a letter to inform an applicant that she/he was unsuccessful in a job application.

8 Make a list of points that might show your employee is unsuitable for the position.

9 Obtain information from ACAS and make a list of the points where ACAS could assist a small business.

10 Explain 'fair dismissal' and its importance to you as an employer.

CHAPTER 5 *The law and the salon owner*

OBJECTIVES

This chapter deals with the content of some of the major Acts which affect the salon owner – the Health and Safety Act 1974, the Offices and Shops and Railway Premises Act 1963 and the 1993 EC directives on health and safety – as well as accidents in the workplace and the correct reporting of them, maternity rights, redundancy and redundancy payments.

Health and Safety at Work Act 1974

The salon owner has a duty to ensure her/his employees' health and safety in the workplace. Various government Acts ensure that the employer knows what she/he must do.

The Offices, Shops and Railway Premises Act 1963 deals with the minimum standards required for premises to operate with such matters as sanitation, cleanliness, overcrowding, ventilation and lighting.

The Health and Safety at Work Act 1974 added to existing legislation and laid down further statutory regulations for hygiene, health and safety. The Act is enforced by the Health and Safety Commission and the Health and Safety Executive. The latter appoints inspectors to do this. However, local authorities are responsible for business premises and shops, and they ensure that the requirements of the Act are met. The Act requires:

THE EMPLOYER TO

'so far as is reasonably practicable' safeguard the health, safety and welfare of all her/his employees.

THE EMPLOYER MUST PROVIDE

a safe place to work, that is;

- **safe** access;
- **safe** equipment;
- **safe** handling;
- **safe** storage; and
- **safe** transport of materials.

THE EMPLOYER MUST PROVIDE

- safety information/training and supervision;
- and publish a written statement (if she/he employs five or more people) of her/his general policy on health and safety, update it when necessary, and bring to the attention of her/his employees.

THE EMPLOYER'S DUTY TO OTHER PERSONS

is to ensure, so far as reasonably practicable, that persons not in employment are not exposed to risks to their health and safety; this includes contractors' employees, self-employed persons and the public.

THE EMPLOYEE'S DUTY

- is to take reasonable care while at work to avoid injury to her/himself and others;
- is to assist the employer in meeting the statutory requirements;
- is not to misuse or alter anything that has been provided to ensure her/his safety.

If the Act is contravened in any part, the health and safety inspector may issue a prohibition notice if there is a risk of personal injury. This could be:

- an improvement notice, which allows a specified time to remedy a fault; *or*
- a prosecution for contravening a statutory provision.

EC directives on health and safety

Six existing EC directives on health and safety which incorporate new provisions came into operation in 1993. The Workplace Health and Safety Welfare Regulations 1992 included three new provisions:

- safe cleaning of windows;
- the protection of non-smokers from tobacco smoke; and
- provision of rest facilities for pregnant and nursing mothers.

The EC directives are designed to update most legislation on health and safety management. They are part of the European Commission's programme of action on health and safety, which is an essential factor in a single European Market. There is one set of regulations for each directive:

MANAGEMENT OF HEALTH AND SAFETY AT WORK

This will set out some broad general duties which will apply to all kinds of work. The aim is to improve health and safety management.

PROVISION AND USE OF WORK EQUIPMENT REGULATIONS

This is designed to tidy up the laws governing equipment. Most work equipment will need to be accounted for and will include everything from a small hand tool to a large refinery. 'Use' will include every aspect from installing, starting and maintaining the equipment.

MANUAL HANDLING OPERATIONS REGULATIONS

This will replace out-of-date, ineffective legislation. A large number of injuries is caused by the incorrect handling of loads. These often result in pain, time off work and, sometimes, permanent disablement. Three key steps will need to be observed:

- to avoid hazardous manual handling operations where reasonably practicable;
- to assess adequately any hazardous operations that cannot be avoided; and
- to reduce the risk of injury as far as reasonably practicable.

WORKPLACE (HEALTH, SAFETY AND WELFARE) REGULATIONS

These regulations will tidy up existing requirements. They will replace several parts of the old law including parts of the Factories Act 1961 and the Offices, Shops and Railway Premises Act 1963.

The regulations will set general requirements in four broad areas.

PERSONAL PROTECTIVE EQUIPMENT AT WORK (PPE) REGULATIONS

These regulations will lay down sound principles for selecting, providing, maintaining and using PPE.

HEALTH AND SAFETY (DISPLAY SCREEN EQUIPMENT) REGULATIONS

This will cover a new area of work activity. Work with display screen equipment can lead to muscular and other physical problems, eye fatigue and mental stress. These problems can be overcome with attention to:

- the type of equipment;
- the working environment; and
- the tasks performed.

Various leaflets on the new legislation, are obtainable from:

> HSE Information Centre
> Broad Lane
> Sheffield S3 7HQ
> Tel: 0742 892345

The Offices, Shops and Railway Premises Act 1963

This Act is linked closely with the Health and Safety Act 1974. The new EC directives in health and safety will affect this Act. The 1963 Act relates to every part of a shop premises, from showroom to stairs and passageways. The new premises must:

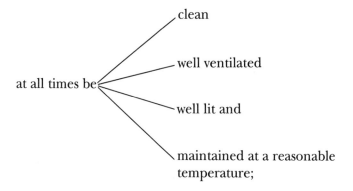

at all times be
- clean
- well ventilated
- well lit and
- maintained at a reasonable temperature;

- have floors, stairs and passageways that are properly constructed, and these must be safe, free from obstructions and properly maintained;
- have fire-fighting equipment and a fire exit which is accessible and unlocked.

The employer must provide:

- clean staff toilets, suitably lit, properly ventilated and easily accessible;
- washroom facilities with running hot and cold water, soap and towels, which are well maintained with adequate lighting and ventilation;
- drinking water and drinking utensils;
- an area for the employees' clothing to be hung;
- an area where food can be consumed;

- an easily accessible first-aid box which contains:

plasters	wound dressing
bandages	safety pins
cotton wool	ointments

The numbers of items in the first-aid box is specified according to the number of staff. It must be easily identifiable and dust and damp free.

Finally, the salon owner must meet the requirements as specified by the local authorities.

REMEMBER

→ have suitable fire extinguishers;

→ check that all gas and electrical appliances are regularly serviced;

→ always make sure that wires, leads and flexes are not left exposed; and

→ ensure that damaged appliances are removed and repaired.

When setting up your salon the local (regional) fire department will give professional advice in relation to your salon's requirements. The department will also check that you have complied with the Fire Precautions Act, in particular the Fire Regulations Act 1976.

Accidents in the workplace

The law demands that accidents in the workplace are recorded. The simple procedure is this:

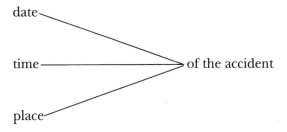

- full name and occupation of the person;
- details of the injury;
- a brief description of the accident.

There should always be an **accident record book** specifically for this purpose. If an accident occurs the *Reporting of Injuries, Diseases and Dangerous Occurrences Regulations 1985* stipulates that employers and self-employed persons must notify the enforcing authority.

If a more serious accident occurs, it is necessary to contact the enforcing authority as soon as possible and within seven days a written report form must be completed and sent to the Health and Safety Executive.

Maternity rights

The Employment Act of 1980 and 1982 and the Social Security Act 1986 allows the expectant mother certain statutory rights:

- to take paid time off for ante-natal visits;
- to complain of unfair dismissal because of pregnancy;
- to return to work after a period of leave due to pregnancy or confinement;
- to receive maternity pay (subject to certain conditions).

The statutory maternity pay the employee receives is claimed back by the employer in the same way as sick pay. Current information can be obtained from the Department of Employment for the booklet, 'Employment Rights for the Expectant Mother', and the Department of Social Security for leaflet NI 257 'Employer's Guide to Statutory Maternity Pay'.

Redundancy

Figure 5.1
Redundancy payments booklet PL808
Employment rights for the expectant mother booklet PL710

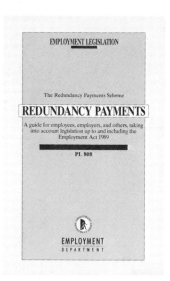

An employee can become redundant when *the employer ceases to trade* or *the employer needs to reduce the workforce.* Employers are required to pay a redundancy payment. The amount varies according to the age of the person and the length of his/her service; generally the employee must have worked for at least 16 hours a week and for a minimum of two years, or eight hours per week for a minimum of five years.

The Department of Employment publishes a leaflet, 'Redundancy Payments' which gives detailed current information.

ACAS

ACAS offers free services to you on matters that relate to employment or industrial relations, and will provide free booklets on many aspects of employment. The head office in London is at:

> Clifton House
> 83 Euston Road
> London NW1 2RB

THINGS TO DO

1 Refer to the Offices, Shops and Railway Premises Act 1963 and consider the importance of:
(a) cleanliness;
(b) ventilation; and
(c) lighting;
as specified in the Act in relation to you as a beauty salon owner.

2 According to the Health and Safety Act 1974, an employer must provide a safe place to work. List the responsibilities you would have:
(a) to your staff; and
(b) to your clients:
if you were an employer.

3 The 1993 EC directives broaden the existing Health and Safety Act. Say how this would affect your staff and salon.

4 Give the reasons for a salon to have an accident record book.

5 List the statutory rights of the expectant mother according to the Employment Acts of 1980 and 1982 and the Social Security Act 1986.

6 Employers are required to pay a redundancy payment. Comment on this as a salon owner.

CHAPTER 6 *The communicator*

OBJECTIVES

This chapter explains the salon owner's role in establishing effective staff and client communications, the skills in handling objections and developing a good telephone manner, and the way to maintain a satisfied clientele.

As a salon owner you are the person who is responsible for good staff relations. You are:

manager
personnel officer
beauty therapist

You have several **major roles** to play and you may need to perfect certain skills and evaluate your own attitudes. **Good listening skills** and **understanding** are vital. A genuine interest in your staff as people and not only as employees is very important.

Communication can be verbal, visual or non-verbal. Body language often conveys a very different message to what is being said, and eye movements can also tell a person exactly what you are thinking. The tone of voice and the manner in which you speak and present yourself is all communicated to the receiver. Ask yourself:

> WILL MY APPROACH BE EASY AND SINCERE
>
> OR
>
> ARROGANT AND DICTATORIAL?

Once you have acquired the best skills your verbal communication will be easy. You must then consider how it will be most effective. (If you feel that you need further assistance in verbal communication there are a number of courses offered by Adult Education Centres. There are also tape cassette courses available from your local library.)

Any instructions should be:

clear
concise
unambiguous

Then they will be understood easily.

Often it is necessary to reinforce instructions, so they should also be written. This will:

help to prevent a mistake
help the person not to forget

Effective client liaison

Enquirers to your salon are potential clients. Therefore, it is important to ensure that your staff are trained continually in good client liaison. It is never wasted. The way your clients are received is most important.

REMEMBER

first impressions count: always welcome your enquirer with your face and voice.

SMILE GREETING

'Good morning'.

IDENTIFY YOURSELF:

'My name is . . .'

OFFER SERVICE:

'Can I help you?'

As the salon owner you know the importance of *visual communication* and *body language*. It is important that your face and body reflect what is being said. Your client will know whether you are sincere.

THE ENQUIRER

is a valuable person – she/he will probably become a client.

REMEMBER

without clients there is *no* business.

If the enquirer wants information she will ask for it.

MAKE SURE INFORMATION IS:

accurate and detailed and answers her/his questions.

Keep it simple:

- speak to the enquirer in language that she/he understands;
- explain the treatments carefully; and

- make sure the enquirer is satisfied with your explanation.

If it is absolutely necessary for you to leave the enquirer, ensure that *you excuse yourself* with politeness and courtesy at *all* times.

Never leave the enquirer too long – return as soon as possible. When you have dealt with the enquirer's needs, check through them again. Does she/he want to make an appointment? If so, make the appointment. If she/he is uncertain, ensure she/he has the salon card and leaflets before she/he leaves.

Bid your enquirer *goodbye* with the same pleasant manner that you greeted her/him.

REMEMBER

she/he is a potential client.

Telephone enquiries

Telephone enquiries should receive the same courteous attention as your caller. *Never* leave your enquirer unattended on the telephone.

REMEMBER the enquirer cannot see you. Your voice is the only contact that she/he has.

When your enquirer becomes a client she/he deserves:

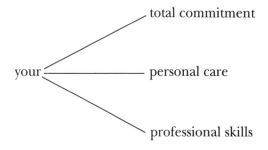

your — total commitment

your — personal care

your — professional skills

REMEMBER effective client liaison is achieved by:

- respect;
- consideration;
- skilled work;
- a genuine interest in the client.

> **LISTEN**

to her/his needs carefully and sensitively.

> **NEEDS**

plan her/his treatments so that her/his needs are met and you have given the best advice.

> **RESULT**

a satisfied client.

Consider your own problems before you start work – then, as a true professional, put them aside. The client does not come to the salon to hear extra problems – she/he will probably have enough of her/his own.

Salon treatments offer your client:

- a temporary opportunity to escape from problems;
- the chance to be pampered;
- permission to unwind and relax.

Make sure your client can do this.

A satisfied client:

```
                    returns
                       |
            speaks well of the salon
                       |
              speaks well of you
                       |
           recommends you/the salon
                       |
              keeps you in business
```

Handling objections

It is always important when handling objections to remember your attitude towards the situation and person.

> **ALWAYS**

be sincere – put your opinion across ensuring that you are not using language which promotes aggression, for example, the use of the word 'you' in this situation is often over-emphasised and is therefore seen as aggressive.

TRY

to reach a solution you are both satisfied to accept.

REMEMBER

your tone of voice and your attitude are important.

CHECK YOUR REACTIONS

they can be:

aggressive: 'Have you?', and
passive: 'Well . . . I don't know.', or
assertive: 'What is the problem, can I help?'

We know that clients are *not* always right, though they would like us to believe that they are. In the beauty profession it is vital the client receives the treatment that is correct for her/him. Occasionally, clients want a treatment that is unsuitable. How will you advise your clients?

There are many ways of handling this, but first you must be convinced that the treatment is unsuitable:

The sincerity of your approach is important because it is necessary that the client trusts your opinion.

Your professional expertise.

You might start by **identifying** and **empathising** with the client: 'I can understand why you would like . . .' and then emphasise why the treatment is unsuitable and positively suggest an alternative.

Emphasise the **benefits** of the alternative treatment:

- how it will meet the client's **needs**; and
- its suitability.

Do not be too 'pushy'.

Keep a steady, even voice explaining the best treatment for her/him. If the client feels comfortable with your explanation and advice, she/he will either say or communicate her/his feelings non-verbally, for example nod her/his head.

Finally ask if you can go ahead. This method works only if you practise it well and genuinely believe that you are giving the client the **best advice**. The client will recognise this.

If you offer alternatives without a good reason, often you will lose a client because she/he will feel pressured into agreeing with you.

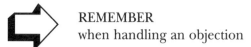 REMEMBER
when handling an objection

empathise with the client
|
identify with the client
|
offer a solution
|
wait for the client's agreement

THINGS TO DO

1 Draw a chart to show how good communication skills can achieve good results in the salon.

2 Show how you would answer a telephone enquiry. Create a role-play situation.

3 Write a short dialogue to show how you would handle an objection from a client regarding her/his choice of beauty treatment.

4 A good rapport is important when dealing with clients. List ten points that show how you would establish a good rapport with a client.

PART 3 *Your business*

CHAPTER 7 # *Purchasing or renting your business*

O BJECTIVES

This chapter looks at purchasing or renting a business; the location of the business and the specialist advice that you may need to seek; the type of property you might choose; and what you need to look for when you think you have found the 'right' premises.

You have made the decision to become your own boss:

- You can *buy* your salon in a town, the country, or at a resort.
- You can *rent* a salon in the above places or in an *hotel.*
- You can be a *mobile* beauty therapist.

See Chapter 19 for more information

Location

If you buy your salon/business what must you consider?

- Where will it be?
- How will you decide?

The position of your salon can be the difference between success and failure.

Businesses are advertised in local or regional advertisers. This will show you what is available and give some idea of the prices. Then you will need to talk to a **commercial estate agent**.

The commercial estate agent will be able to offer information about the businesses that are 'for sale' with his company and also give general advice, for example, council application for a change of use, if you wish to change the nature of the existing business.

Check the area you have chosen. Are there any proposed development plans for:

new businesses?

housing?

You will probably consider an area you know well so that you are familiar with the local amenities. Does it have:

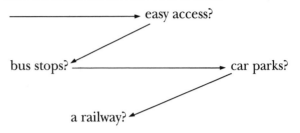

Is it:

- near to other shops?
- a successful area?

If you are starting from scratch, you must be sure there is a market for beauty therapy. You may need to consider some *market research.*

If buying an existing salon, you will want to check carefully the salon's financial history. Is the trade increasing or decreasing? You will want to check with local authorities and the environmental requirements.

CAREFUL CHECKING AND GROUNDWORK CAN SAVE MAKING A MISTAKE.

Type of premises

What type of premises will you buy:

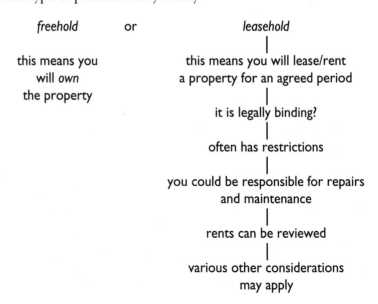

Professional advisors

When buying a business you will need:

- A *surveyor* to be sure you know the value of the property. A full structural survey tells you about most aspects of the property, including plumbing and electricity.

  Valuations are a necessary expense. You can save yourself a lot of money by obtaining accurate information from them. You can also be advised about fire requirements which may not have been updated in the property. This is information of vital importance.

- An **accountant** to advise you on the **vendor's** (the person selling) accounts, and financing your business.

- A **solicitor** to advise on the legal terms of a contract and to transact the business contract, when you decide to buy.

When you find the business you intend to purchase, you will want to examine the accounts of the vendor to evaluate the business and the price that is being asked. The accounts will show what expenditure has to be made and what income there has been. They will show:

THINGS TO DO

1 Check out local papers/commercial estate agents/property advertisers and find the cost of
   (a) renting a salon;
   (b) buying a salon;
   in your area.

2 Carry out some market research (design your own questionnaire) in your area, as if you were intending to buy a new salon.

3 Investigate the cost of professional fees for
   (a) a solicitor;
   (b) a surveyor;
   for business transactions when buying or renting a business.

4 Imagine you are preparing to rent a small business. Make a list of names and addresses of people that you would need to contact.

CHAPTER 8 *How to finance your business*

OBJECTIVES

This chapter deals with financing your business and the various options that you may consider to raise capital. It explains the importance of a business plan and the need to have some personal security. The value of partnerships, limited partnerships, limited companies, and sole trading and franchising are considered.

Once you have decided to buy your own business you will need to consider **finance**. If you have personal savings to invest this could be a good start, but where will the balance come from?:

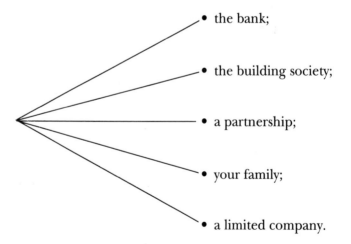

- the bank;
- the building society;
- a partnership;
- your family;
- a limited company.

Your accountant will advise how much you will need to borrow, then you need to look at your options.

The bank

Any of the major banks will expect you to prepare a detailed business plan so that they can see if your venture is worthwhile. The plan should show full details about:

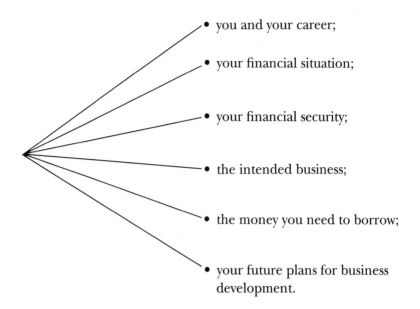

- you and your career;
- your financial situation;
- your financial security;
- the intended business;
- the money you need to borrow;
- your future plans for business development.

Banks can offer more than just a loan or a mortgage. They offer financial advice and services which are of benefit to the business owner. Some banks offer their own package and business start-up guide, which give ideas, advice and guidelines to setting up and operating a small business. It includes preparing your business plan. Check with *all* the banks to see what is on offer.

The bank may offer you a commercial mortgage or a loan. A **mortgage** is usually a long-term loan with regular monthly payments, including interest; a **loan** can be short- or long-term with regular monthly payments, including interest. A bank will usually expect you to offer some security for a loan so that it knows its money is safe. It will also expect you to invest an equal amount into the business or property.

 REMEMBER

the business plan is very important.

The building society

The building society can offer mortgages on business property but this is not an easy option to pursue. It is necessary to contact individual building societies to see what facilities are available.

Partnerships

This can be very useful when establishing a business if one person or several people (up to 20) wish to invest.

Points to consider:

> each partner is responsible for the other's debts;
>
> each partner shares the profits;
>
> individual goals and ideas may vary;
>
> you need to know the person(s) very well.

If a partnership is formed, it is not absolutely necessary to have a written agreement, but it is strongly advisable. Your solicitor will advise you and prepare the agreement.

LIMITED PARTNERSHIPS

This type of partnership protects the individual in the agreement. A partner(s) is only responsible for debts to the total that she/he has put into the business – but one partner must accept unlimited liability. The limited partner has no management powers, but she/he does share the profits and does have a right to see the accounts. A limited partnership must be registered with the Registrar of Companies.

The family

Someone in your family may wish to assist in financing your business, either in a private capacity or in a partnership. The arrangements would be made between the two of you and probably an agreement drawn up by your solicitor.

A limited company

This could be set up when you have established your business. A limited company is when two or more persons want to own the company. They are the **shareholders**. A limited company may be **private** or **public (plc)**.

A **private company** does not offer shares to the public. A **plc** offers shares to the public. A limited company must be registered by the Registrar of Companies. For more information and registration forms contact:

(England and Wales)
Companies House
Crown Way,
Maindy
Cardiff CF4 3UZ
Tel: 0222 388588

(Scotland)
Companies Registration Office
100–102 George Street
Edinburgh EH2 3DJ
Tel: 031 2255774

(Northern Ireland)
Companies Registry
IDB House
64 Chichester Street
Belfast BT 4JX

Franchising

This is not really a way of financing your business, it is an alternative business proposition. Franchising is when a *patent organisation*, the **franchisor**, establishes a format for operating a business. The franchisor establishes:

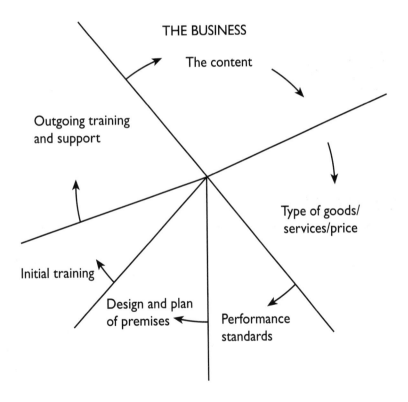

The franchisor then 'sells' the package (the franchise) to a business person (the franchisee). The franchisee pays an initial fee and a percentage of his profits. There is:

professional management expertise of a
business system

|

training and on-going support

|

the complete package for the salon

|

advertising

|

restricted freedom in the business

|

percentage payments to the franchisor
can be costly.

If you consider a franchise always discuss all aspects of it with your solicitor and make sure your Franchise Company has a good track record and is a member of the British Franchise Association.

So there are several options open to you. If you decide to go it alone with no partner, you will become a **sole trader**.

There are many ways in which you can obtain free advice:

- government schemes have been set up to help small businesses;
- TECS (Training and Enterprise Councils);
- local enterprise agencies and the DTI's (Department of Trade and Industry) Enterprise Initiative;

All offer current information and advice for new businesses.

THINGS TO DO

Obtain a 'property advertiser' and find:

1 A business for sale – imagine you intend to purchase or rent it. Itemise the procedure you would use.

2 Draw up a business plan that you could present to a bank in order to obtain a loan.

3 There are advantages and disadvantages to a partnership. Imagine you are considering this and make a list of the pros and cons.

4 You need to raise £10,000 for setting-up your salon. Consider where you might go to raise the finance, how much interest you will pay, and for how long you will have the loan.

CHAPTER 9 · *Business insurance*

OBJECTIVES

This chapter deals with business insurance for buildings, contents, employer's liability, public liability and product liability.

Buildings and contents insurance

Your business will need to be *insured* whether you own or rent it. If you own the business, you are responsible for:

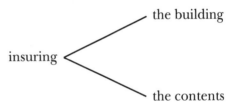

Insure the **building** against:

Insure the **contents**:

These all must be insured against the same perils as the buildings.

Insure the **people**:

staff
|
customers

You will need **employer's liability insurance** and **public liability insurance**.

Employer's liability insurance

This protects you, the employer, against any claims brought by an employee who may get injured on the premises. You must have employer's liability insurance and the certificate must be displayed in the salon.

Public liability insurance

This protects you in case a member of the public is injured on your premises.

Product liability insurance

This is also a very essential part of your insurance. Make certain it is included in your policy. It will protect you against claims arising from products which are not necessarily the manufacturer's responsibility and which may be your responsibility. If a product is being used in a claim as unsuitable there are many aspects that have to be checked and every person involved with the product can be held responsible. Product liability insurance helps to alleviate this by protecting the retailer/therapist.

A recognised broker (who will belong to the British Association of Insurers) will advise you on the type of insurance that is appropriate to your business. A broker will also 'shop around' to find you the best policy.

Alternatively, you can contact an insurance company directly and it will send a commercial insurance consultant to advise you and give a quotation most suited to your business. You will pay a premium for your insurance protection, either annually or monthly by cheque or direct debit.

Insurance premiums are high, but are a necessity and can protect:

yourself
|
your business
|
your staff
|
your clients
|
your future

NEVER ECONOMISE ON INSURANCE

 Make sure that:

your policy is index-linked
(rises per annum according to the level of inflation)
|
you have a 'new for old' policy
(this covers the replacement cost of your articles)
|
your policy suits your requirements

Figure 9.1
Hairdresser's liability booklet
Retailer's combined insurance
proposal booklet

THINGS TO DO

1 Obtain information from a commercial insurance company on the type of insurance package that it might offer to a small business. Compare this package with another company and decide which company is offering the best deal.

2 It is important to have a policy that is index-linked. Comment briefly on this statement.

CHAPTER 10

Keeping business records

OBJECTIVES

This chapter explains the details of keeping business records, whether you manage your own accounts or have accountant. It deals with your day-to-day expenditure and income, and the necessary records you must keep for yourself and the Inland Revenue. More advanced bookkeeping and an accountant will be required as your business develops and you will need to forecast your cash flow.

Your accountant can produce a profit and loss account and a balance sheet, and will submit your accounts to the Inland Revenue. You will register for VAT when your business has reached an annual turnover of £37,500 (this figure can change annually).

Unless you are qualified in business accounting, it is always advisable to let your accountant advise you on procedure. Ultimately she/he will prepare your accounts to send to the Inland Revenue as you will have to pay tax on your profits.

Your accountant can show you how to record the daily business. There are many accounting book systems available, and it may be that your accountant will prefer you to use one of these. By keeping accurate records you will be able to monitor the business and its development.

Bank accounts

You will need to open a separate bank account for your business. You will need a cheque (current) account and a deposit (savings) account

A cheque account will provide for your regular payments. A deposit account will enable you to save money for your income tax and accountant's fees. With your new accounts will come a detailed business guide for the small business.

Expenditure and income

You will need to keep details of your:

expenditure and income

Keep:

receipts
|
cheque book records
including cancelled cheques
|
bank paying-in book
|
bank statements
|
invoices

Expenditure such as:

rates
|
rent (if applicable)
|
heat
|
energy
|
insurance
|
postage/telephone/stationery
|
advertising
|
product
|
travel expenses
|
wages
|
bank charges
|
accountant's fees
|
salon expenses, for example, towels/gowns

Cash books

You will be able to start simple accounts and will need to keep a **cash book**. A simple way to record the day's takings would be to use a **sales receipt book**, either a duplicate book – or a book with a stub (so you have a copy).

For example:

Figure 10.1   *Sample sales receipt*

Sales receipt	Sales receipt
1 hour	1 hour
b/massage	body massage
£23.50	£23.50
Date: 26.9.93	Date: 26.9.93
No. 200	No. 200 VAT included

A simple **income cash book** could be drawn up like this:

Figure 10.2   *Sample income cash book*

Date	Sales receipt number	Detail		Amount	Output VAT
		Product	Service		
26.9.93.	200		Body massage	£20.00	£3.50

An **expenditure cash book** like this:

Figure 10.3   *Sample expenditure cash book*

Date	Invoice No.	Cheque No.	Details	Total Amount excl. VAT	Input VAT
26.9.93.	TF 12650	0061252	Couch	£200.00	£35.00
26.9.93.	Petty Cash	0061253	Postage	£4.00	–

You may want to make this system more detailed by adding further columns after the VAT. These would be *'analysis'* columns so that you can see easily the different areas of expenditure of income. For example:

Figure 10.4   *Sample expenditure analysis columns*

Input VAT	Stationery	Postage	Heating	Product
				(and so on …)

or:

Figure 10.5   *Sample income cash analysis columns*

Output VAT	Massage	Type of Services		
		Facial	Waxing	Manicure

This analysis is a good guide to how your business is progressing. It shows the popular services and products and the areas you need to consider for promotion. At the end of each week or month you can add up your income and expenditure. You can check all this information against your bank statement

You will also need a **petty cash book**. This shows your expenses for everyday small items, for example, postage. You should keep your petty cash records in the same way as your expenditure cash book. The petty cash money you will draw by cheque and show in the expenditure cash book.

Figure 10.6   *Petty cash slip*

PETTY CASH VOUCHER

AUTHORISED BY	RECEIVED BY	AMOUNT	
DATE	DESCRIPTION	£	p
		TOTAL	

CAMBRIDGE
REF. D71972

A **SPICERS** PRODUCT

Bank reconciliation   The only differences are usually payments or income that may not have gone through your bank account at the time of the statement, but they will show on your records.

When you have balanced your books, you will compare your findings with your **cash flow forecast** for the month. If there is a large difference in your calculations you will need to analyse the figures carefully in order to reduce expenditure.

Cash flow forecast

This considers the changes that will take place with the cash available in your business – the balance of money in your bank account. The dates that invoices are paid can affect your cash flow at the bank. If you consider your income and expenditure in advance, you are able to see the times when your cash flow is low and you can **plan ahead**:

 You may ——————— reduce purchases during these months

arrange an overdraft for this period

The cash flow forecast helps you to prepare monthly in order to maintain your business.

Bookkeeping

As a business progresses, a more advanced method of calculating income will be necessary. You are able to purchase a *complete bookkeeping package* if you own a computer. There are several types of these on the market, but it would be advisable to check with your accountant before buying one to ensure the package suits your needs.

If you decide to keep records manually or employ a bookkeeper, you will need to be familiar with various stages of bookkeeping. You will need to keep a **sales day book**. This shows an individual record for each class of business or business customers.

A **purchases day book** shows an individual record of money/ invoices you owe to business suppliers. The information from these **day books** is transferred to **ledgers**.

THE LEDGER

This is a system which uses double entry bookkeeping. Sales are recorded on the left-hand side of a page and payments received on the right-hand side. It demands good bookkeeping skills and is best recorded by a professional.

SALES LEDGER

This has all the information from the sales day book.

PURCHASES LEDGER

This has all the information from the purchases day book.

A GENERAL (nominal) LEDGER

This brings both ledgers together and is divided into sections such as:

- debtors;
- creditors;
- bank balance;
- sales.

From this information your accountant can calculate various information. She/he can **forecast profit and loss**. This is how your business will achieve:

- the **sales** it will make;
- the **costs** it will have;
- the **profit** it will receive.

Your accountant can produce a **trial balance**. That is a list of debit and credit balances from the Ledger.

Your accountant can produce a **profit and loss account**. This shows the profit or loss made by a business over a set period of time.

She/he can produce a **balance sheet**. This gives an accurate total financial position of the business on a set date. The balance sheet shows:

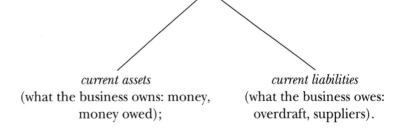

current assets
(what the business owns: money, money owed);

current liabilities
(what the business owes: overdraft, suppliers).

Profit and loss

Figure 10.7   *Sample trading and profit loss account*

Trading and Profit and Loss Account for the Period 1 May 1992–30 April 1993

Sales   £   £

Purchases ─────────────────────────────▶

Opening stock ────────▶

Less Closing stock ───▶

– – – – – – – – – – – – – ▶

Gross profit – – – – – – – – – – – – – – ▶

This balance is taken from the **Sales** and leaves the **Gross profit**

(Rent) and rates ───────▶

Light and heat ────────▶

Wages ──────────────▶

Telephone ─────────▶

Postage/stationery ───▶

Advertising ──────────▶

Travel expenses ──────▶

Bank charges ────────▶

Accountancy fees ────▶

Depreciation ────────▶

─────────▶   ─────────▶

This total is taken from the **Gross profit** and leaves the **Net profit**

Net profit

Figure 10.7 shows that the profit and loss follows on from the trading account. First you have the:

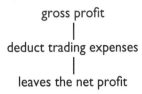

gross profit
|
deduct trading expenses
|
leaves the net profit

The balance sheet

Finally your accountant will draw up the **balance sheet**. Your balance sheet is made up of several parts:

> **FIXED ASSETS**

are items necessary for the business to function, that is, fixtures/ fittings, equipment, motor vehicle

> **CURRENT ASSETS**

are stock that you hold – money in the bank, cash in hand

> **CURRENT LIABILITIES**

are short-term debts, interest on loans, overdrafts, unpaid bills.

The figure for net current assets is reached by taking your current liabilities from your current assets. The net current assets is then added to your fixed assets to give your total assets. The trading account shows the gross profit for the same period.

HOW WILL YOUR ACCOUNTANT CALCULATE THIS INFORMATION?

At the end of your financial year when the accountant draws up the trading profit and loss account, she/he will:

total your sales
|
put your opening stock
(beginning of year) with
your purchases, then
|
deduct stock left over at
end of year (closing stock)

Figure 10.8   *Sample balance sheet layout*

Balance sheet

These depreciate in value each year and an allowance is made for this in the profit and loss account and it is shown on the balance sheet.

Fixed assets		Cost	Depreciation	Balance
Fixtures/fittings equipment				

Current assets

Stock

Debtors

Cash in hand

These are deducted from the above to give the *net current assets.*

Less   *Current liabilities*

Creditors

Bank overdraft

These are added to your *fixed assets* to give your *total assets*

(add to)

Net current assets

Total assets

Represented by

Capital

This is the *opening financial position*

The profit from the profit and loss account is then added 'Drawings': this is the money you personally draw from the business, depending on your trading situation, for example, sole-trader.

Opening capital

(add) Profit for year

Less drawings

Schedule D tax

When your accounts are submitted to the Inland Revenue the profits of your business, as a sole-trader, are liable for income tax.

This Schedule D tax is payable on the profits. You will pay this tax half yearly.

VAT (value added tax)

This is a tax on goods and services. You have to register for VAT if your annual turnover (annual sales) is liable to exceed £37,500 (current rate). This level can change annually, so you will need to check with your VAT office. The present percentage of VAT is $17\frac{1}{2}$ per cent and this is added to

- products;
- services.

Some products are exempt, for example, food.

If you pay VAT:

you will register with the Customs and Excise Office

 you will send monthly or quarterly VAT payments (returns).

How VAT works

- it is charged on your products and services (**output tax**); and
- it is paid on your purchases (stock and equipment) – (**input tax**).

When sending your VAT return to the Customs and Excise, you will subtract the **input tax** from the **output tax** and the balance only is sent. If the **input tax** is higher than the **output tax** you may claim this back.

VAT RECORDS MUST BE KEPT CAREFULLY AND ACCURATELY.

VAT return

The VAT return is issued by the Customs and Excise. The main columns are input VAT and output VAT. The VAT return:

- summarises the totals of input and output VAT;
- arrives at a balance that will either be for the Customs and Excise or the salon owner.

If payment is due to the Customs and Excise, this must be paid promptly and by a set date after the end of the tax period, if not penalties and interest are charged.

Customs and Excise requires:

 accounts to be kept and these must be available when a VAT officer calls to examine them. Regular checks are made.

Your local VAT office will advise you of the procedure for VAT registration, or where to apply for registration. General details can be obtained from:

Customs and Excise
New Kings Beam House
22 Upper Ground
London SE1 9PS

THINGS TO DO

1 You will need a business account. Find out the differences between a business account and a private bank account.

2 Check out two packages and business guides offered by two high street banks.

3 Create a page in an income cash book showing ten treatments (services) completed at a salon in a day. Total the day's income.

4 Create a page in a daily petty cash book showing expenditure for five items.

5 Explain briefly:
   (a) cash flow forecast;
   (b) profit and loss;
   (c) trial balance;
   (d) balance sheet;
   (e) current liabilities;
   (f) fixed assets;
   (g) net current assets.

6 Draw up a page in your daily income cash book to show how you would record output VAT.

7 Explain the purpose of the VAT return.

CHAPTER 11   *Keeping business records – employing staff*

OBJECTIVES

This section deals with the financial responsibilities you have when employing staff. The Inland Revenue requires you to issue a pay advice slip and make deductions of income tax and National Insurance (NI). This information is recorded in a wages book.

A P.45 form must be issued when an employee leaves. There are four classes of NI contributions and this can be paid to the Department of Social Security weekly or monthly. Statutory Sick Pay must also be paid if the employee has been sick for four or more consecutive days.

You and your staff may consider a personal pension plan. This qualifies for tax relief and allows you to plan for your future.

Where to get advice

When you start in business, there are always places that you can obtain information. Your local tax office publishes a booklet, IR 28 'Starting in Business'. This offers basic advice and helpful guidelines. The Inland Revenue also publishes a leaflet, IR 53 'Thinking of Taking Someone On?'. This may be useful to obtain when you want to employ staff. It advises you about deducting income tax under the Pay As You Earn scheme.

Wages record book

When employing staff you will need a **wages record book**. The employee will receive a pay advice slip which you will either give to her/him with her/his wages, or if you pay directly into her/his bank account, you will give the employee a pay advice on its own. A pay advice slip could look like the one below:

Figure 11.1 *Sample pay advice slip*

PAY ADVICE SLIP	
Name	
Week No .... Date	
Basic pay	£
Overtime	£
Commission	£
Bonuses	
Total gross pay (before deductions)	£
Income tax	£
NI	£
Other	£
Total deductions	£
Total net pay (after deductions)	£

You should record all the details in the **wages book** – it will be required by your accountant.

Income tax

The Inland Revenue (IR) publishes two useful leaflets: IR 53 'Thinking of Taking Someone On' and IR 34 'PAYE – Pay as you Earn'. As an employer you are responsible for operating PAYE – you will:

- inform the tax office when your employee starts;
- deduct tax from your employee's wages according to 'tax-tables' supplied by the IR;

- pay the tax deducted to the IR monthly;
- complete the tax cards issued by the IR which record all the information relating to your employee's wages;
- tell the tax office when the employee leaves your employment.

When your employee leaves you will complete **Form P.45**. This shows:

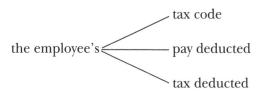

throughout the year she/he has worked to the leaving date. One part of this form goes to the tax office; the other part goes to the new employer.

TAX CODES

All employees under the PAYE system are issued with a tax code. If your employee has been previously employed she/he will give you a P.45 which will give you this information. If not, she/he must apply to the tax office for a code.

The tax code gives one certain allowances. Everyone is entitled to a **personal allowance**. This is the amount they are allowed to earn before paying tax. It is usually raised each year in the government's budget. For example if your allowances are £3,445 (the current single person's allowance), your code would be 344. A letter usually follows this code: L is a common one and it includes the personal allowance for those aged under 65.

National insurance

When you employ people you are responsible for paying their wages and also deducting income tax and national insurance (NI) contributions. NI contributions go towards a state retirement pension and the National Health Service.

You or your accountant can work out how much NI must be deducted by the tables supplied by the Department of Social Security (DSS). Refer to: DSS 'Small Employer's Relief', NI 278, and Quick Guide – NI, NI 268.

if you are a sole trader you will have
to pay Class 2 NI contributions

|

if your business is a company, then you are
an employee and you will pay Class 1 contributions

|

if you employ staff, then they will pay Class 1
contributions if they earn more than £54 per week
(current limit)

WHAT YOU NEED TO KNOW

There are *four* classes of contribution:

CLASS 1

This is paid by employers and their employees between the age of 16 and retirement.

CLASS 2

This is a 'flat-rate' amount paid by self-employed people. Class 2 contributions do not entitle the self-employed person to any state benefits, only the flat rate state basic pension.

CLASS 3

These are voluntary contributions paid at a flat-rate per week. These are available for people who have paid too few Class 1 or 2 contributions to qualify for state benefit.

CLASS 4

This might also be paid by the self-employed person if her/his taxable profit is over a certain amount (check current legislation). This additional payment is assessed and collected by the Inland Revenue. Only half of the Class 4 contribution is payable as tax relief is given on the other half.

A CERTIFICATE OF EXEMPTION

This can be applied for (in advance only) if you think that your earnings from self-employment will be below £3400 (1992–93).

HOW TO PAY NI

NI can be paid monthly at a Post Office or by direct debit from a bank account.

Statutory sick pay (SSP)

When employing staff you must pay a minimum level of sick pay to most employees aged 16 or over. If they have been off sick for *four* or more days in a row, you:

- pay SSP like normal pay;
- can claim back 80 per cent of SSP each month from your NI contributions or tax payments.

For current rates refer to DSS:

SSP Tables 55
SSP Manual (NI 270)
Quick Guide SSP (NI 268)

available from your local DSS who also operate an advice line for employers on Freephone 0800 393 539.

Figure 11.2   *Quick guide to National Insurance, statutory sick pay and statutory maternity pay*

Personal pension

As a salon owner you will want to plan for your retirement. A personal pension will enable you to do this. A further incentive is the tax relief that you are eligible to claim if you pay income tax. You may also want to help your staff with this.

Quite simply, the benefits of a personal pension plan to you are:

$17\frac{1}{2}$ per cent of your earnings can go into
your pension plan (more as you get older)
|
the government allows you tax relief which
goes into your personal pension plan
|
you can choose to retire from the age of 50;
at retirement you can have a tax-free
lump sum (a specific amount), and
|
a weekly/monthly pension

There are numerous pension plans available – check them out to find the best one for your needs. Free advice and information can be obtained from various companies.

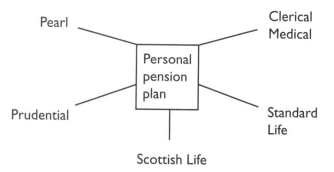

THINGS TO DO

1 Complete a sample pay advice slip showing the necessary deductions.
2 Under the PAYE tax system, an individual is given a personal tax code. Find out how this is calculated.
3 As a salon owner, which class of NI contribution would:
(a) you pay;
(b) your employee pay.

4 From where would you obtain advice on sick pay?
5 From where would you obtain advice on tax codes?
6 From where would you obtain advice on NI?
7 Obtain details of a personal pension plan from two companies.
8 List the advantages of a personal pension plan.

CHAPTER 12 *Staff training*

Objectives

This chapter explains the importance of primary accounts and money transactions that your staff will need to know in order to assist in running your business. A working knowledge of purchase orders, delivery notes, goods received notes, invoices, credit notes, debit notes, statements of accounts is given. The importance of keeping accurate stock records for stock turnover and annual stocktaking is also explained.

Money transactions – cash, cheque and credit cards – require different handling, and staff need to be proficient in making accurate transactions. The Cheques Act 1992 makes payment by cheque safer than before.

Effective salon records

If they are to assist you well in the running of your business, your staff will need to be familiar with the following:

purchase orders
|
delivery notes
|
goods received notes
|
invoices
|
credit notes
|
debit notes
|
statements of account

A regular weekly session could be the best time to offer on-going training in your salon. You might prepare sample sheets and keep them in a training manual. *Keep it simple.*

A PURCHASE ORDER

is when you complete a form to buy products from another supplier/company.

DELIVERY NOTES

or a goods received note is given to the salon when goods ordered are delivered. Delivery notes should be checked carefully with the products to make sure they have all been delivered. Sometimes the delivery note may not show all the articles if the supplier was out of stock. The products should also be checked to make sure they are in good condition. The receiver usually signs a delivery note; a copy of this is kept by the receiver and one by the person delivering the goods.

When the goods have been delivered:

THE INVOICE

will be sent. This is a bill and must be checked against the delivery note and then paid. Many suppliers allow up to 30 days' credit.

A CREDIT NOTE

is received when there has been an overpayment at some time and the supplier is advising you of this.

A DEBIT NOTE

is when the salon owes the supplier. When a salon buys from a particular supplier on a regular basis, the salon will have an account with the supplier. The supplier will issue a statement of account at the end of each month.

A STATEMENT OF ACCOUNT

will show:

- the amount that has been **ordered**;
- the amount that has been **paid**;
- the amount that is **outstanding**.

Invoices

An invoice might look like this:

Figure 12.1   *Sample invoice*

A. Supplier

Any Industrial Estate

London NW3 4JP

Sales Invoice

To:	A. One	**Invoice No:**	183476
	A. Salon	**Date:**	10.12.93
	Anytown	**Terms:**	30 days
	KT13 4PW		
Date order despatched		9.12.93	

Quantity	Description	Unit price	Total price
10 x 200 ml	Oil of Evening Primrose	£4.00	£40.00
10 x 100 ml	Cucumber Mask	£3.00	£30.00
	Sub total		£70.00
	VAT @ 17½%		£12.25
	Total		£82.25

Stock turnover

This is an important factor in your business:

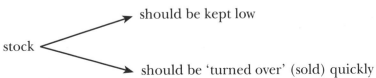

stock — should be kept low

stock — should be 'turned over' (sold) quickly

When the stock is sold quickly, cash is available and your money is being used properly. Your daily analysis in the cash book will show you the products and services which are selling well. If sales fall, then you must reduce your stock purchasing as well.

Stock records

Stock can be recorded when your order arrives simply by keeping a stock record book. An example of a **simple stock record**:

Figure 12.2   *Sample stock record book*

Date	Supplier	Received	Balance	Sold
12.6.93	Breens order No. 22	12	18	6

Every category of produce will have a column and information from your purchase records will ensure it is accurate. Similarly, records of sales are necessary.

 Accurate records of sales and purchases are needed for your end-of-year accounts and you will have to stocktake for this purpose.

If you use a computer in your salon, this information can be recorded on a regular basis. The computer package you use will:

- record the information;
- calculate your stock;
- forecast your requirements.

Stocktake

You will be required to *stocktake* your stock assets for your accounting year. This means that you will have to count your stock and value it. If a computer package is used, this will be a simple matter of pressing a few buttons and the results will appear if you have accurately recorded up-to-date information.

If you undertake this task manually, it can take a considerable time. However, if your stock control record books are kept up to date, this will save time and energy.

Money transactions

Your clients will pay by:

- cash;
- cheque;
- credit card.

Your staff should be proficient in handling all these transactions.

CASH

This is the simplest transaction as long as the therapist/ receptionist is proficient in giving change. Many cash registers will advise you of the amount of change due.

CHEQUES

The Cheques Act 1992 aims to make cheques safer as a means of payment by reducing fraud. It advises that cheques crossed with the words: 'Account Payee' or 'Account Payee only' ('A/C Payee' or 'A/C Payee only') cannot normally be transferred to another person. Such a cheque must be paid into an account in the name of the person named in the 'pay' section of the cheque. Your staff will need to check these points:

- the date should be correct;
- the cheque should be made out to the retailer;
- the amount in words should match the amount in figures;
- the cheque must be signed by the person paying;
- the client should have a current cheque card which guarantees the cheque up to a certain limit, for example, £50 (the bank does not have to honour a cheque above this amount);
- the card also shows the client's signature and the cheque card number should be written on the back of the cheque (by the therapist/receptionist).

If these points are checked, then your payment by cheque will be received.

 Remember → check now, payment later
miss now, *miss out!*

CREDIT CARDS

Access and Barclaycard/VISA are two well-known credit cards. Access is provided by the London Clearing Banks and the Royal Bank of Scotland, and Barclaycard/VISA by Barclays Bank. These services cost you – the retailer. As a service charge, you pay a small percentage of the value of your sale. The salon owner also pays a sum to join the scheme. This can be expensive for you when starting your business.

- The client who uses the card gains a period of credit.
- You present the bill to the bank and you receive payment.

There are still manual machines for processing payment by credit card and your staff would need to be proficient in carrying out a transaction, but these are generally being replaced by automatic transaction machines, where the credit card is inserted and details are checked and cleared at a central point. The transaction is then processed by the cash register and the completed details appear on the credit card sales slip.

THINGS TO DO

1 You are making a staff information manual for use in your salon. Prepare a few sample pages, clearly and concisely, showing some of the information you would include.

2 Design a stock record card that you might use in your salon.

3 Design a flow chart to show the main points of the Cheques Act 1992 that you could display by your cash register to assist staff when checking cheques.

CHAPTER 13 *Staff and appraisal*

OBJECTIVES

This chapter explains the importance of regularly monitoring staff performance through appraisal. Appraisal means that the employer can identify training needs, assess job satisfaction, target goals, highlight problems, develop good communication skills and understanding. The employee has the opportunity to evaluate her/his performance, discuss problems and career aims and to feel valued. The appraiser will need to use good communication skills and an objective, honest, open approach in order for the appraisal to be meaningful. An appraisee performance form should be completed by the appraisee and appraiser for future appraisals.

Well-conducted appraisals can improve staff relations and assist in identifying an individual's needs, performance, strengths and weaknesses. They assist you – the salon owner – in identifying training needs, skill shortages, employees' needs and your salon's needs.

In the 1990s, industry has become very aware of the importance of training and career development. If your business is to meet and maintain high standards of professional expertise, it is necessary to employ motivated staff and to keep them motivated.

The *purpose* of appraisal is to monitor an employee's performance:

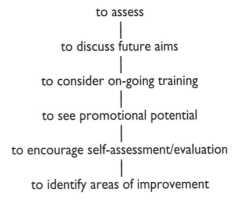

to assess
|
to discuss future aims
|
to consider on-going training
|
to see promotional potential
|
to encourage self-assessment/evaluation
|
to identify areas of improvement

Regular appraisals mean that you are aware of the performance levels of your staff and, therefore, you can be ahead of any problems.

Your employee will be able to:

- discuss problems;
- air grievances;
- discuss her/his career aims;
- discuss her/his strengths and weaknesses;
- measure her/his performance;
- see that you take a personal interest in her/him.

As an employer, you will be able to:

- improve communication skills and understanding;
- identify staff training needs;
- assess job satisfaction among staff;
- discuss the strengths and weaknesses of staff;
- target goals for the future;
- highlight areas that need attention among staff;
- offer constructive advice and praise to staff;
- show your employees that you care and are interested in their career development.

As an employer how you **approach** the appraisal is very important – you should **value** the opportunity to **talk** with your staff and **listen** to their **needs** and **identify** their strengths and weaknesses and their career aims.

You should use an easy approach to accomplish this. If you are a 'good' employer, true appraisal is operating continuously. A few periods set aside throughout the year would be to discuss points in depth.

Your manner needs to be:

- honest;
- positive;
- objective;
- open;
- friendly;
- calm;

so that your employee is encouraged to talk freely.

If you know that some of your comments might not be favourable, you should make sure that you:

state any problems clearly
|
always back up with facts
|
ask for reasons
|
listen
|
agree on action

You should also ensure when you conduct the appraisal that:

- there are no interruptions;
- you have full employee information available;
- you concentrate on problems/situations that can be improved;
- you agree on an action plan and target;
- you identify training areas which may be needed to achieve certain objectives.

An appraisal form should have information you think necessary to monitor progress. A few useful guidelines are suggested in Figure 13.1, however, the appraisal form could be more spacious:

An appraisal interview takes time – ensure sufficient time is allowed. A well-conducted appraisal can improve staff relations and will assist your employee in her/his development and assist you in the running of your salon.

Appraisals help to develop **your staff**

 Developing your staff is *identifying*

their needs
|
performance
|
weaknesses
|
strengths
|
needs for training

Successful, satisfied staff work well and develop your business.

EMPLOYEE PERFORMANCE ASSESSMENT

Name of appraisee: *Assessment scale* 1–5 ☐

Job title:

Date started: **1** Poor–does not meet requirements of position

Date started in present position: **2** Below average–improvement necessary

Date of last appraisal: **3** Satisfactory

Date of appraisal: **4** Very good

Date of next appraisal: **5** Excellent

Areas to be assessed

Communication skills: Clients, Staff, Relationships, Manner

Appraisee   1–5 ☐   Appraiser   1–5 ☐
Comments   Comments

Job performance skills: Services, Sales, Accuracy

Appraisee   1–5 ☐   *Appraiser*   1–5 ☐
Comments   Comments

Figure 13.1   *Sample Employee Performance Assessment Appraisal form*

Personal application: Timekeeping, Attendance, Appearance, Drive,
Attitude, Confidence, Job Satisfaction

Appraisee   1–5   *Appraiser*   1–5
Comments   Comments

AREAS FOR DISCUSSION

Appraisee comments   *Plan of action*

Future career plan

On-going training or support training   *Review date*

Additional information

Appraiser comments

Training and development plan

Objectives to be achieved   *Signature appraisee*

Signature appraiser

Appraisals assist *you* to identify

areas for training

|

skill shortages

|

problems – before they get too big

|

your employee's needs

|

your salon's needs

THINGS TO DO

1 Design an appraiser's form for use in your salon.

2 Create a role play situation of appraiser and appraisee.

3 List the qualities of an appraiser.

CHAPTER 14

Salon layout and design

OBJECTIVES

This chapter explains salon layout and design. There are companies that can assist you with planning your salon. When setting up a salon, consideration must be given to the reception area, staff areas, store rooms, therapy rooms, changing rooms, heating and ventilation, showers and toilets as well as colour schemes, floor covering, fixtures/fittings and equipment.

Where to get advice

There are companies who will advise on salon layout. This is often free of charge if you purchase equipment from them.

HOF (House of Famuir) offers salon planning on the basis of a fee, currently £70 + VAT. HOF produces a suggested layout based on:

- the size of salon;
- what you envisage in the salon;
- the type of treatments intended;
- the number of therapists, and so on.

HOF does not produce architectural drawings, as these are a matter for the salon owner's builders/architects. If and when the client purchases the salon equipment from HOF, the original fee is refunded.

Some other companies which give informal advice on equipment and planning are Ellisons and Taylor Reeson. The George Solly Organisation offers formal and informal advice.

DON'T FORGET, LOOK AROUND AND SEE WHAT COMPANIES CAN OFFER YOU.

Figure 14.1   *Suggested layout for beauty salon and massage room (submitted by HOF)*

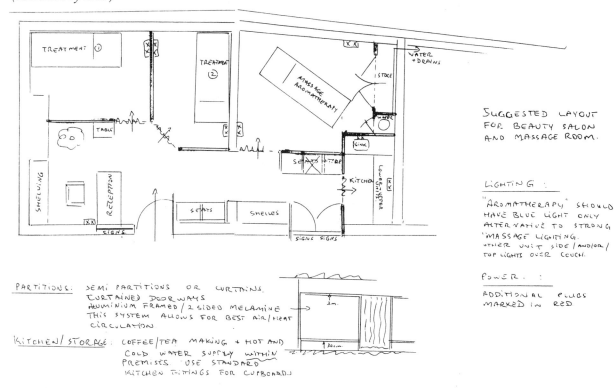

Figure 14.2   *Suggested layout for beauty salon (submitted by HOF)*

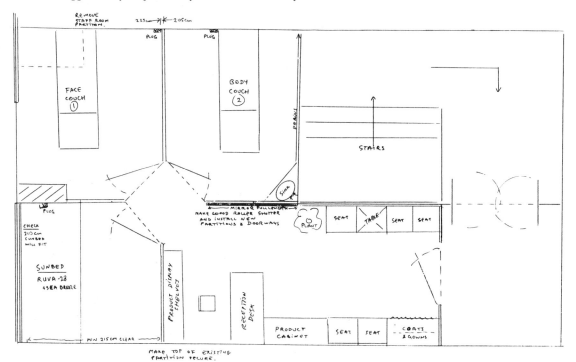

Figure 14.3   *Suggested layout for beauty salon (submitted by HOF)*

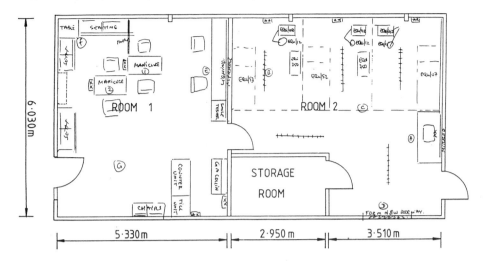

Setting up the salon

Planning your salon means that you must consider:

- staff comfort and efficiency;
- your clients' comfort;
- meeting current legislation, that is, various Acts which stipulate how you operate your working environment.

The salon layout is often dependent on the existing plumbing. You may wish to change this or add to it – it will depend on your financial budget. Once you have organised your 'wet' areas, you will want to consider your layout.

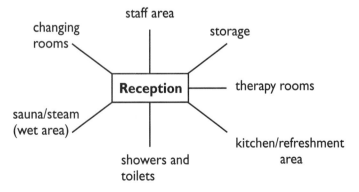

The most important area of a salon is the reception – it is where your client arrives. If this area is dull, uninteresting, crowded and your client is badly received, she/he will not return. Your reception area will need:

comfortable chairs
|
a table
|
product display units
|
a magazine area
|
product information
|
surrounding decor, for example plants
|
a reception desk
|
a cash register
|
an appointment book/telephone
|
a price list
|
any relevant client information
|
soft background music

You will need to have a suitable area here to place the client's coat. Your client needs to feel welcomed and made at ease as quickly as possible.

Your **business registration certificate** should be displayed in the reception area if you are a limited company, so should a **disclaimer notice**, that is to show that you cannot take responsibility for the security of clients' property. It is also compulsory to display **a list of your charges**; your diplomas and your staff's diplomas should also be exhibited. The changing rooms should be discreet and private, that is, not in view of the reception area, and the beauty therapy rooms will require:

electrical points
|
space
|
cupboards
|
shelving
|
lighting
|
equipment

You will need to be able to move comfortably around the couch, and all equipment should be easily accessible and be able to be used safely. You should also have products displayed so the client can see and ask about them.

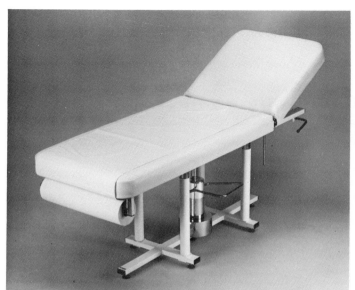 

Figure 14.4   *Essential salon equipment*

Lighting needs to be adaptable; you will need soft as well as bright lighting, depending on the treatment being offered. Mirrors are a useful asset, but careful placement is important.

Decor

The *colour scheme* for the salon will be dependent on your own taste, but it is good to consider:

- colours that will not date;
- colours that harmonise and create a relaxed atmosphere.

Good colour co-ordination will please any age group. Pastel colours are popular for this reason. Advice on colour and fabric matching can be obtained from department stores. Changes in colour schemes can be quite simple if you consider this at the beginning.

Hygiene is vital in the beauty salon and your *floor covering* will receive a lot of attention. It needs to be:

- comfortable to stand on;
- non-slip;
- hardwearing and able to withstand floor cleansers.

Good flooring is expensive but necessary if it is to meet the demands of everyday use. Carpet is not a good idea for beauty therapy rooms, although it is attractive for your reception area.

Fixtures, fittings and equipment

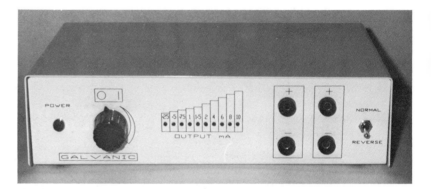

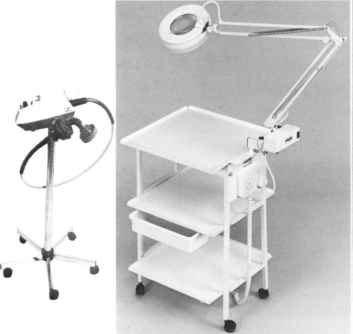

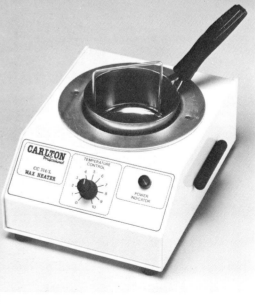

Figure 14.5   *A selection of equipment for salon use*

You will need to consider these carefully and will probably change your mind a number of times. For this reason it is important to ensure that your fittings, where possible, are adaptable and that some equipment is portable so that maximum output is possible. Seek advice from the professionals and consider your own particular requirements before you rush into this area of planning. Equipment needs to be:

- reliable;
- repairable.

Check with suppliers if they offer:

- a repair service;
- a free loan while an item is being repaired.

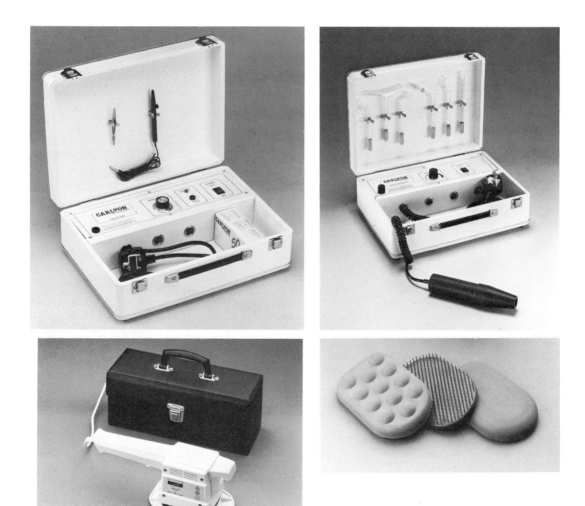

Figure 14.6   *A selection of portable equipment*

Second-hand equipment

This can be useful for 'furniture' requirements, including tables, couches and stools. New electrical equipment comes with a guarantee – this must be considered when setting-up a salon.

Cost is also a key factor. Before you buy:

- check out the wholesalers;
- check out the equipment;
- check out the service.

Store room

This should be an area that is easily accessible for staff, but not near client areas. It should be:

- secure;
- have adequate shelving;
- fulfil your needs.

A storage cupboard would be used for products and items for everyday salon use, such as:

- client gowns;
- towels;
- couch rolls.

This cupboard needs to be accessible but not necessarily in public view. It needs to be well-maintained at all times. Large salons may choose to have small storage cupboards in each working area.

Heating and ventilation

This is necessary if your salon is to function properly and to comply with legislation. Seek professional advice on efficiency and performance.

REMEMBER
The salon can generate a lot of heat with various treatments and an even temperature is desirable for working therapists and client comfort.

Staff area

This should be designed according to current legislation.

Toilet facilities

It is necessary to consider separate toilet facilities for staff and clients.

Client comfort

When considering client comfort, give them the feeling of luxury and being pampered. Think about:

- changing rooms;
- toilets;
- shower areas;
- steam baths;
- saunas.

A salon that has been designed carefully allows the client to progress from changing room to treatment area with a simple, on-going progression in a relaxed, private environment.

Refreshment area

This is subject to the Food Hygiene Regulations and local authority Environmental Health Act. You may choose to use a vending machine or to serve your clients. Personal attention and the use of cups and saucers is still favoured by many clients as 'elegant', giving them the feeling of luxury and being pampered. You must consider all aspects when making your decision to serve refreshments:

hygiene
|
cost
|
space
|
clientele

The salon's exterior

This needs to be **attractive**. You may want to have:

- a new canopy
- your own sign and logo

What you want and what you have will depend on:

- your budget;
- council legislation.

REMEMBER
always check legislation before you make plans.

The interior of your salon will develop as you decorate and furnish it. Then consider finishing touches:

- silk flower displays;
- plants;
- a music system.

The latter can set the scene for a relaxing environment, and should be gentle, quiet and not obtrusive. Loud, dominating music will not be conducive to a relaxed environment.

If you play music in a public place you must have a licence. For information contact:

Performing Rights Society,
33 Berners Street
London W1P 4AA

THINGS TO DO

1 Find out the requirements of your local authority for setting up a beauty salon.

2 Design a salon layout for a room 9 m × 5 m to include a changing cubicle area and reception area. Consider:
   (a) colour scheme/decor;
   (b) flooring;
   (c) lighting;
   (d) equipment/furniture.

3 Make a list of the minimum equipment you would need if you were working alone in a small salon. Cost the equipment and consider what manufacturers/wholesalers can offer you.

CHAPTER 15 *Running your salon*

OBJECTIVES

This chapter explains the various aspects of running your salon. It considers buying stock and the advantages and disadvantages of buying products from wholesalers, manufacturers and cash and carry wholesalers. Your product range, how to select a product and the advantages of producing 'own-brand' products are covered. The services you offer your clients will be largely dependent on the skills of your staff.

The daily operating requirements of your salon revolve around cash handling, security, banking, cleaning and laundry and salon maintenance. Costing and being cost effective are important and must be taken into account at the initial planning stage. The salon owner must also be aware of certain legislation as laid down in the Consumer Protection Act 1987, Supply of Goods and Services Act 1982, Resale Prices Acts 1964 and 1976 and Trade Descriptions Acts 1968 and 1972.

Buying stock

Stock can be bought from:

wholesalers/suppliers   manufacturers

cash and carry
wholesalers

Wholesalers/suppliers advantages:

- sell a wide range of products;
- often, there is no minimum order;
- may offer monthly terms (30 days' credit);
- will deliver your materials.

Cash and carry wholesalers advantages:

- allow you to buy what you want when you want it; *but*

Cash and carry wholesalers disadvantages:

- you may be tempted to buy more because of product display;
- you have to go and buy it.

Manufacturers send out representatives and they only sell their own company products. They might offer:

- sales literature;
- up-to-date information with their products;
- demonstrations in your salon (usually free of charge);
- a minimum order value;
- training with their products;
- a credit period (30 days).

There are a number of points to consider when you buy stock. A credit period can assist your cash flow, and 'buying as you go along' can be useful when you are budgeting.

CONSIDER THE BENEFITS THEN DECIDE ON THE BEST METHOD FOR YOU.

Figure 15.1   *Cash and carry wholesale facilities*

Selecting your product range

This is a very important area to consider. It needs time and patience. You may be fortunate to have worked with a professional range of products and already decided that you will use that range. If not, what must you consider?

Most products have a **selling life** span. The new product is:

introduced → its demand grows

|

its demand matures

|

its demand declines

Some products will sell longer than others but, eventually, manufacturers of a successful range of products will feel that the range must be:

- re-energised, and so the range is increased.

This means that:

- old products are faded out; and
- new ones take their place.

There are advantages and disadvantages to this, but manufacturers know their work. They can:

- offer you an efficient service; and
- meet your needs.

 You will need to look around and investigate the market. Consider:

The cost to you of salon products.

The cost to your clients of retail products.

Your profit margin.

The more expensive the product, the greater your profit margin will be. Make sure:

 your products are client affordable.

Many companies will offer you a **launch pack**. This might consist of:

- a full range of retail products (one of each);
- a full range of salon products (one of each).

In addition, you may receive *free of charge*:

- salon promotional literature;
- client product leaflets;
- a selection of product samples;

- a product manual;
- posters;

and free posting and packaging and 10 per cent discount on the launch package price.

A launch package could start at around £600 for a moderately priced product. There are plenty of product companies. Make sure that you obtain lots of:

- information;
- free advice;
- demonstrations;

before you decide to select a product.

Figure 15.2   *An attractive product display*

Producing your 'own-brand' products

This can be prestigious for you if you find a good company that produces 'own-brand' products, and you like the quality of the product. Own-brand products mean:

- you have a professional identity;

- you will have a higher profit margin;
- a good reason for selling.

If you decide to consider this scheme, you will need to test some product ranges first to make sure they meet your needs. Own-brand products can be found in trade journals and at trade shows and exhibitions.

 REMEMBER make sure you insure adequately for product liability. See Chapter 9.

What treatments will you offer?

This will depend on the skills of your staff. Beauty therapists who hold full recognised diplomas will be able to offer all the general treatments. In addition, you may have wisely recruited staff with additional skills such as:

- reflex zone therapy;
- aromatherapy;
- ear piercing;
- nail modelling.

You will want to consider your range of services with the staff and equipment you have available.

Daily requirements

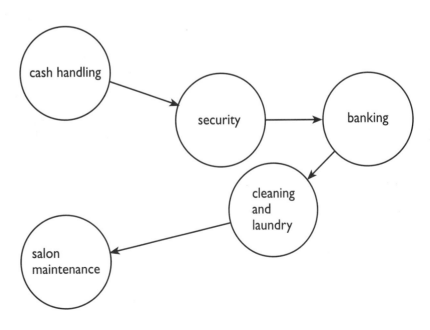

An electronic **cash register** will satisfy many needs. It is:

- secure;
- helps accuracy;
- will show daily income;
- can record and print other information (depending on the model).

If money is kept at the salon it should be secure in a cash register or in a safe. Banking should be done as often as possible for safe handling of money. Your local crime prevention officer will advise you on salon security, such as burglar alarms.

Your salon should be cleaned at least once a day and regular attention paid to any untidiness as it occurs. Everyone is responsible for a clean, safe establishment.

GOOD ORGANISATION IS VITAL

Washing towels and gowns is a regular daily feature. Your *own* laundry service is the most efficient method for maintaining regular supplies, so invest in a good washing machine and tumble dryer.

Just as your salon needs cleaning, it will need to have regular maintenance to maintain high standards for health and safety. Make sure you find a reliable maintenance person. This will be an asset.

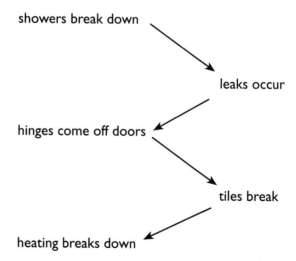

These could be **daily** occurrences in the salon. *Don't wait* until they happen to find a person to fix them.

THINK AHEAD

A drop in standards means
a drop in business

Client records

Wherever you decide to keep your client information:

- on a computer (see page 113, Data Protection Act);
- in a filing box; or
- in a filing cabinet;

ensure that it is never on public display, for example, a record card left on the reception desk. This information is private and confidential and is necessary only for the therapist to perform the best treatments.

REMEMBER leave a file, lose a client.

Confidentiality and professionalism are necessary at all times and reflect **your** standards and the standards in **your** salon.

Figure 15.3   *Record system*

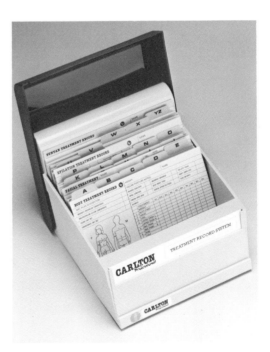

Being 'cost' effective

If you are retailing a particular range of products, the manufacturer will have given you a suggested retail price (SRP). It is a guideline only and you are allowed to charge more or less than the SRP.

Products and materials that you use in the salon will be 'costed' by calculating expenditure and time for the services you offer. Costing is calculated by taking the hourly (monthly) rate for each member of staff and adding your proportional costs to it. You will then:

- calculate the total sum; and

- divide it by the number of working weeks.

This figure will give you the basic amount that must be earned per hour. You must then add your profit.

 Calculate all your expenses to find what you must earn per hour. Then you will be **cost effective** in your salon.

Consumer Protection Act 1987

There are a number of Acts which the salon owner must be aware of that relate to the products that are used and sold. The Consumer Protection Act 1987 aims to safeguard the consumer from products that do not reach a reasonable level of safety. This is particularly important in the salon because of product liability. Part I of the Act deals with product liability.

In the past, injured persons had to prove a manufacturer negligent before they could sue for damages. This Act removes the need to prove negligence. The Act implements the EC directive on product liability, which provides a similar degree of protection for people in the EC.

An injured person can take action against:

producers
|
importers
|
own-branders

Other suppliers, such as wholesalers and retailers, are not liable unless they fail to identify the producer or own-brander if asked to do so by the injured person.

Liability under this Act is not restricted to consumer goods. Goods used at a place of work are included as well as components and raw materials of a product.

Detailed information on this Act can be obtained from:
Consumer Safety Unit
Department of Trade and Industry
10–18 Victoria Street
London SW1H 0NN

Supply of Goods and Services Act 1982

This Act deals with consumers' rights and traders' obligations in England, Wales and Northern Ireland. The Act is in *two* parts:

- Part 1 is concerned with goods;
- Part 2 is concerned with services.

PART 1

This applies to goods supplied:

- as part of a service;
- on hire;
- in part exchange.

This Act extends the protection for consumers provided by the Sale of Goods Act 1979. The goods supplied as specified above must now be:

- of merchantable quality;
- fit for any particular purpose made known to the supplier;
- as described.

The consumer is entitled to claim back some or all of her/his money from the trader if any goods do not meet these requirements.

PART 2

A person providing a service must give the service:

- with reasonable care and skill;
- within a reasonable time;
- for a reasonable charge.

The consumer will follow a particular line of action if there is a complaint:

- first, go back to the supplier if not satisfied;
- second, contact a consumer adviser at a trading standards department.

This Act is very important for the salon owner as she/he should be aware of her/his position as a supplier and as a provider of services.

Trade Descriptions Acts 1968 and 1972

The retailer must not:

- supply misleading information;
- falsely describe; or
- make false statements;

about her/his products or services.

The retailer must not make false comparisons between present and former prices:

She/he should not offer products at half-price unless they have already been offered at the actual price for at least 28 days.

The retailer must also be aware of statements saying that something is 'our price' and it is worth 'double the amount'.

The retailer should be aware that price comparisons can be misleading and are often illegal.

Re-sale Prices Acts 1964 and 1976

These Acts stipulate that manufacturers and wholesalers cannot compel retailers to sell their goods at a fixed price. They can suggest recommended suitable prices.

Suppliers cannot withhold stock from retailers who choose to sell below the suggested price. One exception is that: suppliers can set a price if it is 'in the public interest'.

THINGS TO DO

1 Design a business card and letter heading for a small salon and an attractive leaflet with your price list. Find out the cost of printing this material. Obtain at least two quotations.

2 Write to two product companies and find out what they would offer you in a launch pack if you were setting up in business.

3 Make a list of all the daily requirements that you might have to check if you were a salon owner.

4 A knowledge of the Consumer Protection Act 1987 is vital if you are a salon owner. Make a list of the reasons why you think this to be so.

5 Explain the importance of the Trade Descriptions Acts 1968 and 1972 to a retailer.

CHAPTER 16 *Marketing and promotions*

OBJECTIVES

This chapter deals with marketing – providing your clients with the services and products they need. You may use market research to assess their needs.

There are many forms of promotions you may choose – advertising, mailshots, leaflets, newspapers, national directories, demonstrations and window displays, for example.

A computer could be a useful business aid and could assist you in producing promotional literature, controlling stock, financial forecasting and storing information about clients. You may need to register with the Data Protection Registrar if you store clients' personal details on your computer.

Marketing is about supplying your clients with the services and products they need. It is not just selling services and products to people. It usually means that you have considered the needs of the consumer in your immediate area.

You will have already organised some **market research** to be sure you have a market for your business. Your marketing philosophy is based on having:

goods services/products
|
at the right price
|
in the right place
|
at the right time

Effective promotions means you have conveyed the above to the consumer and she/he will want to come to your salon. Promotions are necessary if the public are to know that your salon exists.

Today there is so much choice available to the prospective client that you must ensure that she/he selects your salon. There are many forms of promotion. Advertising is one.

Advertising

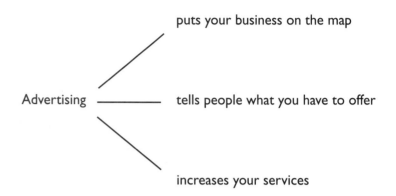

There are many forms of advertising. You will have to decide which form is best for your needs:

CLASSIFIED AND DISPLAY ADVERTISING

Regular classified advertisements in a local paper can be advantageous and not too expensive, and you may be able to have a feature on your salon or your products in a local paper. You may be able to contribute to the paper.

Display advertising can be expensive.

NATIONAL DIRECTORIES

National directories can be helpful to the small business. Some companies, such as Thomson Directories, offer the small business a free advisory package, which includes booklets on general advertising and telephone business, and a cassette tape to assist you in developing a good telephone manner.

Thomson will send representatives to assist you in general advertising planning. It offers a free artwork and design service, and a support service to clients. The prospective client receives a variety of free information and advice in anticipation that she/he will become a client – a good marketing strategy!

Before you buy, check out **free** advice from the professionals.

Figure 16.1   *The Thomson Advisory Package*

LEAFLETS

If you own a computer, a local leaflet drop can be quite inexpensive, and can be a useful way of telling people about your services. A **special offer** or **voucher** attached to this can be an added incentive for the prospective client. However, if you use this method make sure you limit the time that the voucher is valid.

MAILSHOTS

These can also be produced quite simply and professionally on your personal computer (more costly if you have to have them printed). However, postage can be expensive. This could be a good promotional opportunity every few months with existing clients and their friends. You could:

- offer a 'freebie';
- offer a reduced price;
- offer a voucher;
- promote a new service;
- promote an existing service.

DEMONSTRATIONS TO LOCAL GROUPS

Local groups, for example the women's guild, charity groups and church groups, are always wanting speakers or demonstrators. Most salon owners would use this opportunity to:

- meet prospective clients;
- show the services they can offer;
- distribute promotional literature;
- exercise good public relations.

It is an excellent way to meet people, talk to them and invite them to your salon. This gives you the opportunity to:

- promote your image; and
- sell your professional expertise.

There is usually a lot of interest in a demonstration with lots of questions to be answered. Make sure you have the time to talk to people.

 REMEMBER first impressions count.

Stay calm and reflect the professional person. No amount of advertising can make up for the **personal touch**. If you consider large-scale demonstrations:

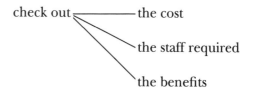

check out —— the cost

the staff required

the benefits

If you have staff who are confident demonstrators and the cost to you is not too high and the benefits are good, then this is a good form of promotion.

Quite often these events can be costly and the return is small – another form of advertising may suit your needs better.

Make-up demonstrations are always popular and you will probably offer a home-visiting wedding service. This can also be a good way of promoting your salon as it allows you to meet many prospective clients. Dress shops and bridal shops are good places to leave leaflets and your business cards.

A bridal package is often used by advertisers to take the strain out of wedding preparations. You might participate in:

- a local advertisement, selling space with printers, hotels, etc;
- join with a bridal shop in advertising.

This can be very productive if your salon is in a busy area and developing good business relationships generates new business. Everyone can benefit from a slice of the cake.

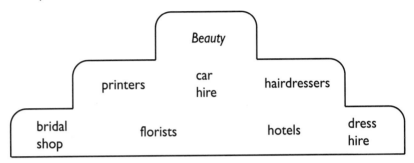

WINDOW DISPLAYS

This is important:

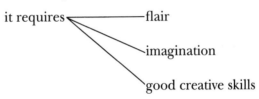

it requires — flair
imagination
good creative skills

Your display must be:

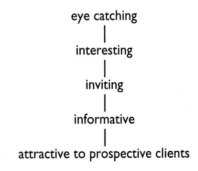

eye catching
|
interesting
|
inviting
|
informative
|
attractive to prospective clients

It will not do this if it is:

crowded
|
dull
|
stale

Promotional literature can obtained from suppliers:

ALWAYS OBTAIN IT, USE IT AND CHANGE IT REGULARLY.

If you cannot produce a good window display, find someone who can! **Plan your** promotions and advertising on a yearly basis:

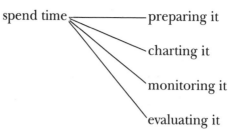

spend time — preparing it
— charting it
— monitoring it
— evaluating it

Keep within your budget.

Information technology

There are many areas in your business where a computer could be used:

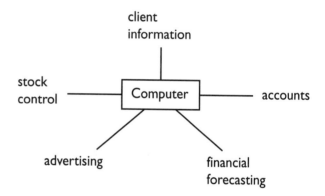

Computer packages can be purchased for basic word processing, which would enable you to produce:

standard letters
|
price lists
|
promotional literature
|
personalised mailshots

You may be concerned that you are not computer literate, but companies today sell inviting programs with their computers. A computer that would answer your salon's needs could cost as little as £1000. Your package could include:

- the computer;
- a personal training package;

- a year's warranty on parts and labour;
- a back-up support service;
- software packages to suit your needs.

The more specialist computer with a colour system and laser printer would be more expensive, but could still be a good investment depending on your salon's needs.

The National Computing Centre – sponsored by the government – offers expertise to the small business. Specialists can offer advice on various types of systems.

Data Protection Act 1984

You may use your computer to store personal details about your clients. If so, you may be required to register with the Data Protection Registrar, which means your business is placed on a public register of data users. You are required to comply with a code of practice:

- to keep the information secure
- to keep the information accurate and relevant to your needs
- to reply to requests from individuals for any information you are holding on them.

Full details and registration forms are available from:

Data Protection Registrar
Springfield House
Water Lane
Wilmslow
Cheshire SK9 5AX
Tel: 0625 53511

THINGS TO DO

1 Prepare a questionnaire in order to carry out market research in your area, on the type of people that use beauty salons and the treatments they prefer.
2 Design some promotional material for your salon.
3 Design a leaflet for a housedrop to encourage new business.
4 Obtain details on the Data Protection Act and list how it affects the salon owner who stores personal details about clients on a computer.
5 Contact your local newspaper and find out how much a small classified advertisement would cost.
6 How much would display advertising cost – consider two examples.
7 What advantages would display advertising offer you?

CHAPTER 17 *Recession*

OBJECTIVES

Recession means that there is little or no growth in industry on a national scale. The country's lack of prosperity is reflected in a drop in consumer spending.

The salon owner must be inventive and resourceful and use all her/his skills during a recession in order to adapt and create business. Adapting to survive is part of business and bankruptcy should not occur if you have taken note of financial forecasting and acted accordingly. Preventative measures in the early stages of recession assist the future.

Any business has to be prepared for the 'bad' times as well as the good. Business will fluctuate throughout the year and you will be able to anticipate the quieter times with your forecast charts.

Recession is different. It means that there is little or no growth in industry on a national scale and, consequently, in prosperity because the country is experiencing financial problems. These problems are then passed on from:

large businesses
|
to small businesses
|
to the consumer

This is the time when all your skill and marketing expertise is exercised.

You must consider services that your clients still need as essential and develop new ones in order to meet different needs. These need not be costly to you. You may consider rent-a-space.

Rent-a-space

When you rent part of your salon to other professional people who may want an outlet for their services – perhaps they can no longer afford to run their own establishment – all of you can benefit from the business. Services that might be considered for a daily rent-a-space could include:

- hairdressers;
- colour analysts;
- osteopaths
- reflexologists;
- chiropodists.

This:

- brings additional treatments to your salon;
- brings new clients to your salon;
- gives you the opportunity to present your services;
- uses space that may not have been fully utilised.

At the same time you must budget your money carefully. Clients are still going to have treatments, they will just be more selective because they are cutting-back and economising.

Economy sales packages could be a good idea. See what your client needs and offer her/him additional benefits by introducing a different free treatment each month. Monitor your results and you can see what is successful. A sample package may be:

Figure 17.1   *Sample economy sales package*

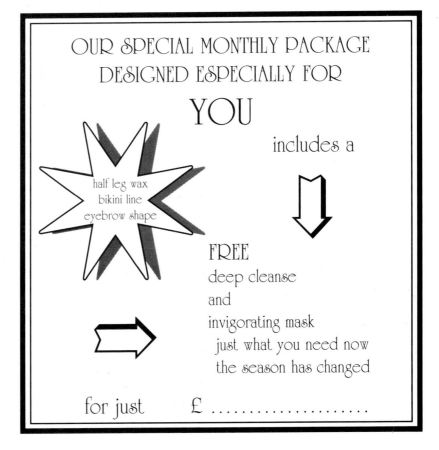

Ask your clients what they would like as a 'freebie'. Design a questionnaire or make a suggestion box. *Listen* to your clients and tailor your package accordingly. It is the best form of advertising.

REMEMBER:

a satisfied client speaks well of you
|
speaks well of the salon
|
recommends you/the salon
|
generates new business
|
returns to the salon

Adapt to survive/expand

If your business has been built on good foundations and you have kept a careful record of business accounts, disasters should not occur:

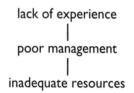

lack of experience
|
poor management
|
inadequate resources

are some of the reasons why businesses collapse. *Never* ignore cash flow problems or a drop in business. Obtain advice from your accountant or bank manager if there are financial problems. **Bankruptcy** occurs when a business **cannot pay its debts**.

A **court** declares a **business** or an **individual bankrupt** on the grounds that it/you is **insolvent**, which means the business is **unable to pay its debts**. A **receiver** is then appointed to take over the affairs of the **insolvent** business/individual.

If you are doubtful about your business, then there are various options open to you. You could:

- sell the business or the lease;
- clear your stock.

Before things get too serious, use your skills and adapt to survive. Use rent-a-space to develop business or to change the face of your present business. The most important factor is to assess what is needed and see if you can supply it.

If you develop your business well and always maintain business accounts, you should be able to take preventative measures in the early stages of any problem:

CUTTING BACK EARLY SAVES CUTTING OFF LATER.

THINGS TO DO

1 Consider how a beauty business could be successful during a recession.

2 Design an economy treatment package to help your business and your client. State how you would promote this economically.

3 Explain how a business becomes insolvent.

4 Explain briefly how bankruptcy can be avoided.

5 List ten points to show how your salon could adapt in order to survive in business.

CHAPTER 18 *Business development*

Objectives

Business development is founded on an awareness of the customer's needs, a knowledgeable approach to services and products and an awareness of business competitors. Business strategy comes from observing, listening and acting upon your findings, targeting your needs and promoting your business accordingly.

Business development is dependent on maintaining and improving the quality of work, and this means on-going staff training and the development and acquisition of new skills.

Creating an excellent salon means that you have professionally established good foundations in many aspects of business and that you must continue to develop, change and discover.

You will no doubt use many forms of marketing and promotions throughout your business life. Initially, and ultimately, the main point is to acquire business. And once you have acquired business you must keep it. Building and keeping clientele is about:

SERVICE: PERSONAL ATTENTION AND BEING AWARE OF YOUR CLIENTS' NEEDS.

You need to be:

knowledgeable about your services
|
knowledgeable about your products
|
aware of your clients – their likes and dislikes
|
aware of your competitors
|
the 'best' for service and personal care

REMEMBER
You cannot buy the personal touch – it has to be established by giving freely of yourself and having a genuine interest in the needs of your clients.

The personal approach

The beauty business is founded on the **personal approach**. Clients can afford to be selective and some are willing to travel miles to receive the sort of attention and service they require.

REMEMBER
build a better business by being better than your competitors. See the *want*, fill the *need*, reap the *benefit*.

Carry out continual client monitoring. Once a month you may produce a questionnaire:

- encourage your client to complete it;
- explain to her/him how valuable the comments are;
- design the questionnaire to be 'open';
- listen to your clients'/enquirers' needs;
- consider what they like and dislike about:
  your salon,
  your services,
  your staff;
- ask if they would recommend your services;

and so on. Good business strategy and business development come from:

observing
|
listening
|
and acting upon your findings

Build your business wisely on your clients':

needs
|
wants
|
benefits

The beauty industry promotes all sorts of products and treatments. You must be discerning. **Not** all clients want **new** treatments all the time. Established treatments performed well with an efficient, friendly therapist who is clean, smart and sincere can mean your clients will return again and again.

Regular custom leads to a good positive business – it also promotes new business as successful salons are sought after salons. Your business development will rely on you considering your existing clientele while promoting additional clientele.

 Target needs → promote monthly services
↓
design packages

for your existing clientele.

Introduce new clients (through the various promotions already discussed) to an:

- introductory treatment;
- introductory package;
- introduce a friend.

Meet their **needs** and they will come and **meet you.**

Skill transmission

STAFF TRAINING – MAINTAINING AND IMPROVING QUALITY OF WORK

The 1990s has brought a great emphasis on training skills, and the standards of industry must constantly be monitored and updated for efficiency. The beauty therapy industry needs highly skilled, motivated people to maintain success in any form of business venture.

Your business can be successful if your staff meets the requirements of the public. Regular weekly staff training sessions will maintain and improve salon standards and procedures.

 Additional training services are vital for new skill development.

Regular training might include:

- new developments in the industry;
- video training/new techniques;
- improving telephone techniques;
- visits to annual exhibitions to keep up to date.

New skill development could focus on:

- management skills;
- public relations;
- marketing and sales;
- advanced aesthetics and therapy.

Many colleges offer post-graduate training courses for the beauty therapist. The acquisition of new skills could benefit:

- your staff;
- your salon.

Leading companies and banks often talk to businesses as part of their service. Your business/staff could benefit from their experience and expertise: banking, accounting and financial planning services are some of the topics that they will talk about.

The importance of on-going training and maintaining high standards will be reflected in a growing industry and a developing business. Your salon will develop and grow with:

expert management
|
skilled, efficient staff
|
excellent services
|
a constant business and client awareness
|
professionalism

Creating an excellent salon means you have built:

yourself
|
your establishment
|
your staff
|
your services
|
your clientele
|
your future

on good foundations and that you are still building, changing and discovering.

THINGS TO DO

1 List five ways that you could find out about your clients' needs.
2 List ten ways you could improve upon your personal service to your clients.
3 Design a promotion for introducing new clients to your salon.
4 Give five examples to show how you would expand your existing clientele.
5 Design an on-going training plan for three staff so that your salon and your staff will benefit.

CHAPTER 19 *Talkabouts*

Figure 19.1 *Natural Woman Salon reception area*

The proof of any theory is putting it into practice! The following interviews relate to many aspects of this book and will be of interest to the prospective business person. Business and beauty therapy is about:

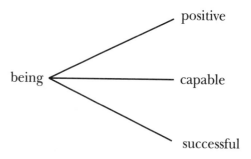

In business, talking to successful people is always a good way of learning the secrets to success. These interviews show how some beauty therapists have tackled the business world.

June's story reveals many aspects of business for the sole trader, including the pitfalls. I first met June in 1988 when I conducted her beauty therapy examinations. I met her again earlier this year and she was well on the road to success.

Interview with June, a high street salon owner

Q **Why did you become a beauty therapist?**

A I had been a hairdresser since leaving school and, after raising a family, continued in hairdressing. I wanted to do more and took a course in cosmetic make-up and electrology. Finally, I found myself on the Beauty Therapy Diploma Course at Kingston College of Further Education. When I qualified, I was determined to establish myself in business. I had some earlier business experience in hairdressing and thought my knowledge and my new skills and positive attitude would be a good start.

Q **So how did you start in business?**

A It was five years ago; I rented a very small beauty room, $1\frac{3}{4} \times 2\frac{1}{2}$ m, within a hairdressing salon in a Surrey suburb. The room had been used for beauty before, but it was a long time ago and there was no existing clientele. The rent was £50 a week and, as my business increased, it rose to £75 a week.

Q **How did you attract your first clients?**

A I decided to introduce myself and my services by providing a manicure service and free skin advice. The personal touch was just what people wanted.

I put an advertisement in the window of the hairdressing salon, which attracted some people. I placed a cinema advertisement, but had no response from this.

Q **How did you select the products you would use?**

A I had worked with Biosthetic Products in hairdressing and decided to use these in beauty. I did not consider looking further because of my knowledge of the quality of the products. It is a skin analysis diagnostic programme with prescription facial products. Biosthetics offer:

- meetings;
- an annual congress;
- a good support service; and
- there is no minimum order (this was an important point for me when I was setting up).

I worked for three years in the hairdressing salon. I worked long hours, but was confident my clientele was growing and it was then I decided to look for bigger premises.

I had numerous difficulties in the room, but having had a professional training, I was able to use my skills to adapt.

Q *What difficulties did you have?*

A I had very little storage space – only a couple of shelves. It was very noisy because of the hairdressing salon. The room had no ventilation and it wasn't always possible to leave the door open.

Q *Did the local authorities approve the room?*

A Yes, because it met the necessary requirements. My problem was trying to maintain a relaxed atmosphere in a small room. I had to stack machines neatly and waxing was always difficult because of the need to move around the couch. I learnt the importance of good hygiene and professionalism.

Q *Was your retail trade good?*

A This could have been better. I couldn't have a display unit because there was no space.

Q *What would you say was your secret to building a good clientele?*

A One-to-one communication was the secret. I gave clients personal attention and I gained new clients through recommendation. When I had established my clientele and my takings were around £500 per week, I decided to move.

I had always managed my own accounts weekly and employed an accountant for annual accounts.

Q *So where did you decide your new salon would be?*

A I knew I wanted to stay in the high street so I went to a commercial estate agent.

I received a lot of information on properties to buy and rent. I decided at the time to rent and soon found an office suite, 545 sq ft, which was located on first-floor premises and had separate front access and entry phone. I decided on first-floor premises because of the high cost of rent and rates for a ground floor shop.

There was a lot to consider – the rent, rates, length of lease and conditions.

I had to apply to the council for a change of use as the premises had been offices. I had to provide:

- four copies of all drawings of the salon's interior layout

- a site plan. The cost of application was £76.

The estate agents were very helpful with advice relating to the local council. I had to wait five months before the application was approved. During this time I could have lost the premises. My licence to operate was just transferred from the other salon.

Q Were there many additional expenses?

A Although I had to employ a solicitor to transact the business, I felt that there was one major point where I had not been advised. The premises have landlords to whom I am responsible, and then there is the freeholder/owner. I was not aware that I would have to pay my solicitor's fees, the landlord's and the freeholder's fees. This was very costly and amounted to £3000.

I leased the property for a term of nine years. My rent is £200 per week and, initially, I had to pay three months in advance; now it is quarterly. The rent is reviewed after five years.

In addition to this, my rates are £59 per week. I am also responsible for paying towards the landlord's building insurance and a proportion of any structural maintenance. I insure the fixtures and fittings and contents. I also insure against public liability.

It is possible for the landlords to elect to levy VAT on rent. This is an important point to check. I did not find out until after I had signed the lease. This is quite an increase on the rent.

Q How did you finance the business?

A I used my personal savings and although I thought I had enough – about £10,000 – £15,000 was a safer estimate. With the recession and high interest rates it seemed sensible to use my personal savings.

Q Was there a lot of renovation and decorating?

A Yes. I found a builder on recommendation and allowed three weeks for all the plumbing, electrics and fixtures to be completed. I found the builder very helpful advising on the plumbing and wet areas.

I wanted to create a very peaceful and relaxing atmosphere in the salon, so I chose a colour scheme of soft greens and peach with cane and pine furniture. I had three beauty rooms, a large reception area, a shower/ steam room and a sunbed.

I bought most of my equipment new, although I would recommend buying good second-hand equipment from a salon or beauty salon that is closing down. I think I would always buy new electrolysis equipment as it carries a manufacturer's guarantee.

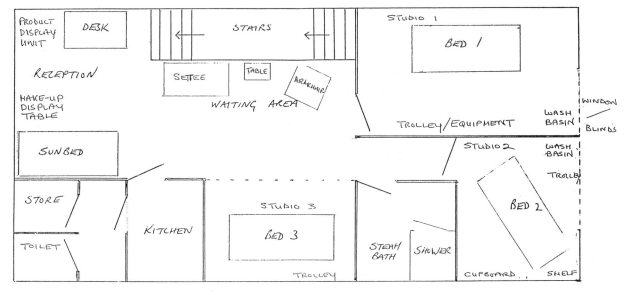

Figure 19.2   *Natural Woman Salon site plan*

I designed each beauty room as a self-contained beauty area and called the salon 'Natural Woman'.

Q   *How did you promote the new salon?*

A   Well, I had my existing clientele and made a leaflet drop. When I had my stationery printed, I had an up-market leaflet printed as well which I hoped people would keep. This has appeared to be so. To date, I have had ten clients from this. I advertised in the local paper, but did not find this successful. It would probably be better with a feature.

I find the main source of trade comes from the 'A' board parked in the street (a free-standing advertising board). Passers-by may pick up a price list from the small box attached to the 'A' board. It is the best £5 I have ever spent!

Clients often introduce a friend by buying a gift voucher as a present. This is a very successful way of developing the clientele.

Q   *Have your sales improved in this salon?*

A   Definitely. I have a good display area and an area for analysing the client's skin. I do not pressure clients and am never pushy but simply advise them about their skin condition. I write out the prescription creams that they would need to buy and tell them to use their own ones and to see me when they have finished them. They always come back. Repeat sales follow on because the product is good and the personal attention is always available. I see the need and satisfy the client.

Q *You bought your lease during the recession; have you ever worried about your clientele declining?*

A No. I am very positive and rely on finding new clients. I have an average of two to three new clients each week.

Q *Now you have expanded, do you still do your own bookkeeping?*

A Yes. I keep accounts simple and my stock control is recorded on a card system. My clients' information is also a card system.

I still employ an accountant for annual accounts. If I keep daily, weekly and monthly accounts it is easy to see where I am and the business is progressing.

Q *How do you staff the salon?*

A I work full time with Anna, my friend and colleague. She is self-employed, therefore, we work independently with our clients; but as a team in the general running of the salon, she has helped me develop the business. We both practise all aspects of beauty therapy, specialising in biosthetic skin care, aromatherapy and reflexology.

I use rent-a-space as a means of income and to complement the beauty. I have a visiting osteopath, chiropodist and homeopath. They pay me a percentage of their takings. We all work towards promoting each others' services.

We have a regular team of beauty therapy students from my former college. They do their work experience in the salon. They act as receptionists and learn to deal with clients. They are also offered in-salon training experience. They receive no payment as it is part of their course. However, I have them in the holiday period also and then I pay them.

This system works well for the college and for me and certainly keeps down staffing costs and gives students valuable experience.

Q *Are there any disadvantages to being a sole trader?*

A Only if one is sick. I cannot afford permanent health insurance; it is too expensive. However, Anna and I help each other so the salon is always covered.

Q *June, you have been trading for 16 months, how do you see your working situation and your plans for the future?*

A I enjoy my work. I don't think of it as work, just my own therapy. I feel I have worked extremely hard to create my beauty clinic. I was restricted by the council when I wanted to put fascia signs outside and boutique-type canopies, but this has not affected my business. I wanted to create a happy, unhurried ambiance and clients frequently comment on the peace and relaxed feeling they find within the salon. They find it a retreat from the stressful life-style that people endure these days. One of my clients says that the salon is 'A Haven in New Malden.'

I am pleased that the clientele enjoys my salon and that they benefit from coming to 'Natural Woman'. I see what they want and I supply the service and together we benefit. There is no substitute for professional skill, good service and genuine personal attention.

When I move again, it will be to buy a salon and possibly to have a partnership. At the moment I am pleased with the way the business is developing.

Interview with Geraldine, a sole trader within an hotel

Q **Tell me why you became a beauty therapist?**

A I trained in beauty therapy when I was 37 years old. Previously I had worked in administration in a computer firm and for a while worked as a legal secretary in the USA. When I returned to England, I took a full-time training at Langley College, now East Berkshire College. I qualified in beauty therapy and electrolysis with the ITEC Examination System.

Before my training had finished, I met a woman who had set up a small beauty room in a large four-star hotel not far from Heathrow Airport. The woman offered me employment when I qualified. I liked the salon/room and the working arrangements. The two of us would operate this room/salon and one in Marble Arch, London. Each had been established within the hotel chain by this lady.

Figure 19.3 *Hotel plan showing location of Beauty Room facilities*

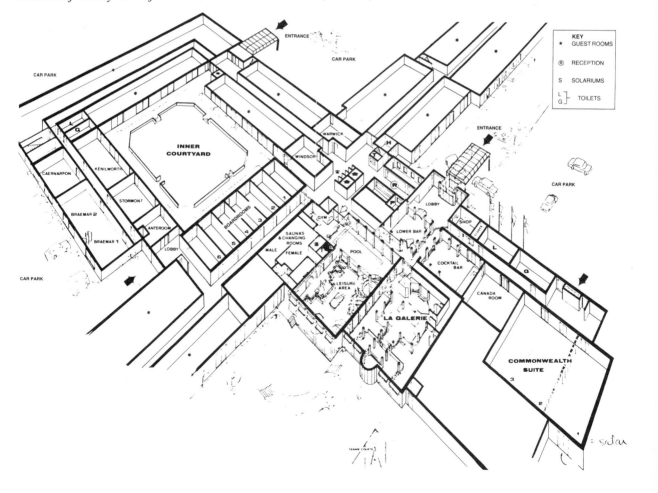

KEY
* GUEST ROOMS
® RECEPTION
S SOLARIUMS
L / G TOILETS

Q *So you went to work for someone else. What were your plans?*

A I made it clear from the start that I would only work for 12 months and then would be looking for a partnership or something else. She accepted this. A year later she decided to go to live in the USA and I bought the business. The goodwill, that is, and the equipment. I had always been trusted with banking and running the salon, so it all progressed naturally.

The room was on a three-year contract with a £10 per annum rent increase. I was able to take over the contract. The hotel wants the facility and they are keen for it to run smoothly. I actually purchased the goodwill of the salon and the salon in its entirety, that is, equipment and products.

Q *How did you finance this?*

A I used my personal savings. The total outlay was around £8,000. I still had to pay the rent to the hotel, but I had a ready-made clientele, about 30 regular clients whom I had got to know throughout the year I had worked there.

Q *Were there any other expenses?*

A I am responsible for the salon insurance and public liability insurance. I pay for my telephone, but have a reduced rate.

Q *Are there any perks or advantages having a room in the leisure complex?*

A Yes, I think there are many. All the towels I use are supplied by the hotel and they are laundered free of charge. The electricity is included in the rent. I have hot and cold water and full air conditioning as there is no window. The room is decorated by the hotel so I have to conform to the colour choice, but it is usually quite attractive.

I also have free lunches, drinks and staff car parking and am able to pay a reduced rate for a weekend holiday break.

The room is not very large, $3 \times 3\frac{1}{2}$ m, but is positioned adjacent to coin-operated sunbeds and in the leisure relaxation area close to the swimming pool and Jacuzzi. I have a lot of passing trade from visitors with this set up.

Q *You inherited the products from your predecessor. Would you change to another range?*

A No, they are well known, respected and give good results. They are moderate to expensive, but comparable in price to others. The product company offers:

- free, on-going training;
- back-up support;

- assistance with their brand name advertising;
- professional advice.

Q *Do you hold a large stock?*

A No. I have always thought it wise to keep low stocks and have regular turnover.

Q *Do you have a good retail product trade?*

A Moderate – I do not believe in being over pushy. My clients wouldn't return if I tried the hard sell on them. I find that if the client needs it, I advise her/him and she/he will usually buy it.

Q *What about other costs?*

A Printing can be quite expensive. I usually have:

- leaflets,
- letterheads,
- business cards,
- price lists,
- appointment cards,

printed and I have just paid £90 for 2,000 small cards to go in the hotel key cards. I will have to monitor the response carefully as this is a new venture.

Q *Advertising can be costly and one must be selective.*

A Yellow Pages was definitely a good idea. I placed a *small* box advertisement in it which cost £400. I had it for a year two years ago. I still get calls from this.

Q *How do you attract new clients?*

A I place price lists in the leisure complex reception area, but most of my clients come from recommendation. People like the personal touch and good service.

Q *Are there any problems due to recession?*

A Yes, I am beginning to notice it more recently. Some of the partners of my clients have lost their jobs and some have just had to cut back. This means to me:

- less regular clients;

- occasional treatments;
- loss of some clients altogether.

The room being small does not allow me to develop other areas. It does mean that it is affordable.

Q *How would you adapt to survive?*

A I would make personal cutbacks. Perhaps only open three days a week so that I could go and do demonstrations and talks to promote the business and, if things were very bad, I could seek extra employment.

Q *Is there anything else you could do to promote the business?*

A Only get out and talk to people. There is not room for anything else. At the moment I am holding even, but recently there has been a definite drop in clients. I had increased the clients by a third, but now it fluctuates drastically. I open from 10 am to 8.30 pm, and there is no restriction on my hours. I have one other therapist who works on Thursday evenings. This is on a percentage basis.

Q *Have you tried to generate business with the hotel staff?*

A Yes, I give a 20 per cent discount, but they abuse the situation and are unreliable. They would book an appointment and arrive late, or not at all. One would hope it could have worked. The hotel use consultants for grooming and make-up.

Q *Do you maintain regular accounts?*

A Yes, it is important and you can see your progress. I have a simple method of accounting and stock control. As the business is small, it doesn't require too much paper work. I am not registered for VAT. My accountant prepares my annual accounts. My client record system is the card method.

Q *Do you offer a full range of treatments?*

A Yes, most things except sunbeds, steam and sauna because the hotel have these.

Q *Do you buy from wholesalers or cash and carry?*

A I buy from both for convenience, whatever suits me.

Q *Are there real disadvantages with this type of salon situation?*

A More recently, I have experienced problems because the hotel chain has been bought out, and the management is thinking of increasing my rent by more than the £10 per annum. This would be a problem because there is only so much a single therapist can do. The output of treatments cannot be increased dramatically. I can only put up the prices which wouldn't be good at the moment.

Q *What are your future development plans?*

A There are no immediate plans, although a decision could be dependent on the rent increase, but later I am probably going to move from the area with my partner. I would then start again.

Q *Would you consider the same situation again?*

A Yes, I like working for myself; I am the only one to profit and I like the hotel situation. The only problem with being a sole trader is illness and holidays. You have to decide to close the salon or take on extra help. I find short-term closing is best.

Interview with Sue, a mobile beauty therapist

Q **What made you decide to 'go mobile'?**

A I had worked for a while in a salon, but had always wanted to work for myself. As I was 28 when I trained, I thought it was time to do so a year later.

Mobile beauty therapy had always appealed to me because I did not want to rent or buy a salon. I wanted the flexibility of working when I planned to do so and being able to adjust my work to suit my lifestyle.

I enjoy travelling from client to client. It is a good way of being fresh and interesting for the next client and it breaks up the day's routine. Sometimes I shop or visit a friend between clients. Anything is possible as long as it is planned in your daily schedule.

Q **Was it expensive to set-up?**

A Yes, but not as expensive as a salon. I tried to buy equipment gradually while I was working. Some equipment is vital. You must have a car, a portable couch, box for materials, record card system, and any equipment you require. I chose a portable G5, an electrical muscle stimulator, a wax unit, make-up kit, manicure box, blankets, couch rolls and other disposable materials. There is also printing to consider. I had leaflets, business cards, appointment cards. About £2,000 covered the essentials.

Q **Did you advertise initially?**

A Well, I knew a lot of people and introduced my services to them at half-price. This was very popular. I chose about 20 people and most of them rebooked. I built an evening business first while I was still working. I never took any clients from my employer. This is not professional practice and should always be discouraged. It contravenes the code of ethics of any professional association. If, at a much later date, a previous client chooses to come to you, that is different.

I delivered leaflets to local businesses and shops and introduced myself where possible. I gave my new clients a complimentary treatment if they introduced me to another client. This was very popular and I still use this method of introduction today. It is much better than putting advertisements in the papers. I feel I know my clients in advance.

Q **Have you kept your clientele?**

A Yes. I saw my clients' needs and I tried to provide them the services they wanted, that is:

- value for money;
- a reliable service in their own home;
- a good service.

When clients rebooked and recommended me I knew my business was going well. By the end of the year I had a steady business.

Q | *What qualities would you say the mobile beauty therapist must possess?*

A She/he must have an out-going personality and be genuinely warm and friendly and be a good listener. The therapist must be patient and understanding and skilled in her/his work and enjoy working alone. She/he must be self-motivated and organised.

There is no one else but you when you are mobile. You must be punctual. Your practice relies entirely on you for success or failure. There is no one to refer to and no one to blame. Your success rests on your ability and personality. You must be prepared to take time out for training and up-dating yourself.

I find mobile beauty therapy a challenge; it spurs me on to achieve greater things.

Q | *Do you offer a full range of treatment?*

A I used to offer everything. Now I tend to specialise in facial and body aromatherapy, reflextherapy and sports massage. I occasionally offer other treatments, but natural therapies have become my specialist field.

Q | *Do you keep your own accounts?*

A Yes, I keep a daily cash-book and collate my outgoings with my income and then my accountant completes the accounts.

It is important when you are self-employed to be very accurate with money. You must save to pay your National Insurance contributions and you must save money to pay for your income tax. This is paid annually when the accounts are sent to the Inland Revenue.

Q | *Do you retail a product range?*

A Yes, it is important to offer your clients a retail range of products to complement your treatments. I don't sell on a large scale, but I sell regularly.

Q | *Has recession made any difference to your trade?*

A No, my clients know the benefits of their treatments. They save or budget accordingly. Many feel it reduces their stress levels, so they afford them. As one client put it, 'It's like buying petrol for the car – it keeps me going.'

Q | *What disadvantages are there?*

A It is miserable unloading your equipment when it is raining, but the only serious one you can think of is being ill. You must consider this and save some money for emergencies. You can take out insurance for sickness, but it is expensive and it usually only operates after a month's sickness. I cannot afford this so I save a proportion of my earnings for emergencies.

Holidays are not really a problem. You can select your dates and advise and book your clients around the dates.

Q | *What advice would you give to someone thinking of going mobile?*

A Make sure you are self-motivated, organised and like working alone. You need to know yourself well and enjoy promoting yourself and your business.

Glossary

annual percentage rate (APR)   The annual rate of interest charged on a loan. The APR must be clearly stated by all lenders – banks, building societies, finance companies.

appraisal   To monitor an employee's performance.

appraissee   The person being appraised.

appraiser   The person conducting the appraisal.

balance sheet   A statement of the assets and liabilities of a business at a particular point in time.

bankruptcy   A court can declare an individual or business bankrupt on the grounds that it is insolvent (unable to pay its debts). The affairs of the insolvent person or business are put in the hands of an official receiver.

business plan   A plan which shows your business ideas and activities in detail and predicts the expectations of the business for the year. A business plan is necessary to support an application for a loan.

capital   The total assets of an individual or business, that is, cash, property and other assets.

capital investment   An investment of money into a business for equipment that is permanent or semi-permanent.

cash book   A daily record of payments and receipts.

cash flow forecast   An estimate of a business's cash incomings and cash outgoings over a particular period, for example, six months to a year.

contract of employment   A written or unwritten legally binding agreement between an employer and employee.

credit note   A supplier issues this when there has been an overpayment.

creditor   An individual or company to whom money is owed, for example, suppliers and the bank.

current account   An account with a bank that enables you to write cheques for payment of your bills.

current assets   Assets in the balance sheet which can easily be converted into cash, such as stock.

current liabilities   Liabilities in the balance sheet which show money owed, for example, a bank overdraft. These are short-term debts.

debit note   This is issued by a supplier when the salon owner owes money.

debtor   An individual or a firm that owes you money.

delivery note   When goods have been received by a salon, a detailed note will accompany them from the supplier.

Department of Social Security (DSS)   Government department that deals with social benefits – National Insurance, sickness and maternity.

deposit account   A savings account with a bank that enables you to deposit money and pays you interest.

employer's liability insurance   This insurance protects the employer from any claims made by an employee injured on the premises.

exempt goods   Goods or services which have been declared exempt from VAT (VAT is not payable on them).

fixed assets   Property or assets in a balance sheet which cannot quickly be converted into cash, for example, freehold properties and fixtures.

fixtures and fittings   Equipment that is included in the sale of a business. This is usually itemised in an inventory.

franchise   A licence to trade in the name of another company, usually for an initial premium and regular commission on sales.

gross profit   The profit a business makes before deducting operating expenses, such as overheads and depreciation on equipment.

input VAT   This is paid on your purchases if you are registered for VAT.

insolvency   This is when a firm or individual can no longer pay debts as they fall due.

invoice   A bill for goods supplied on credit stating the goods supplied, the date they were supplied, the cost, VAT if applicable and the supplier's terms.

job description/job specification   A written summary of an employee's title and tasks.

lease   An agreement for a firm or individual when renting (leasing) property for a stated period of time. The individual or firm is the tenant or lessee. The landlord is the lessor.

leasehold property   A tenant holds property under a lease – the tenant does not own the property.

ledger   A system which uses double-entry bookkeeping.

liabilities   Amounts owed by a business to others.

limited company   When two or more persons own a company. They are the shareholders. The limited company may be private or public.

manufacturer   A company who makes a product or equipment.

market research   Researching an area, service or product in order to find out information.

National Insurance (NI)   This is the national scheme for paying for state benefits. Premiums are weekly or monthly and are based on wages or salaries paid. It is the employer's responsibility to deduct NI and to pay the premiums to the Inland Revenue.

net pay This is the 'take home' pay after deductions have been made.

net profit This is the profit of a business after all expenses and deductions have been made. Tax is payable on this.

output VAT This is charged on goods and services if you are registered for VAT.

overheads The everyday operating costs of running a business.

partnership A business association of between two and 20 persons.

pay advice slip Details of gross pay and relevant deductions to arrive at net pay. Employers are required to issue this.

Pay As You Earn (PAYE) The employer is responsible for deducting NI and income tax from employees' pay.

personal allowance The amount an individual is entitled to earn before paying tax.

planning permission Legal permission must be obtained from the local authority in order to change the use of a property or to change its structure.

product liability This insurance protects the retailer against claims resulting from products which are not the responsibility of the manufacturer.

profit and loss A record of the profit (or loss) made by a business over a stated period of time.

public liability insurance This insurance protects the retailer if a member of the public is injured on the premises.

purchase order A form that is used to buy products from another company.

recession When there is no growth in industry on a national scale.

Schedule D tax This is payable on the net profit of your business when your accounts have been submitted to the Inland Revenue.

sole proprietor/trader A person who owns and runs a business on her/his own.

statement A written reminder of outstanding amounts owed (often monthly).

stock Goods held for re-selling.

stock-take This is required annually for your accounts and it means that the stock must be counted and valued.

stock turnover   This is when stock is sold quickly (turned over) and cash is available.

trading account   A summary of sales for a period, usually a year, together with the costs of sales for the same period showing the resulting gross profit.

trial balance   A list of debit and credit balances taken from an accounts ledger.

value added tax (VAT)   A tax on most goods and services in the UK.

VAT return   A form which records details of VAT paid or received by a retailer – it must be completed quarterly and sent to HM Customs and Excise.

vendor   The same as seller, for example, of a property.

wages record book   A record of all wages paid by an employer and required for accounting purposes.

wholesaler/supplier   One who buys goods in bulk and sells in smaller quantities to retailers.

Further reading

Armstrong, M, *Personnel Management*, Kogan Page, 1979

Atkinson, P E, *Achieving Results Through Time Management*, Pitman, 1988

Brewer, Roy, *Do-it-Yourself Advertising*, Kogan Page, 1991

Collins, Helen, *Human Resource Management: Personnel, Policies and Procedures*, Hodder & Stoughton, 1993

Cook, Sarah, *Customer Care*, Kogan Page, 1992

Cox, Roger, *Retailing*, Macdonald and Evans, 1993

Davies, Barry and Davies, Eric, *Successful Marketing in a Week* , Hodder & Stoughton, 1992

Dudley, Jim, *How to Promote Your Own Business*, Kogan Page, 1987

Health and Safety Executive, *Essentials of Health and Safety at Work*, HMSO, 1990

McAral, Daphne, *Croner's Reference Book for the Self-Employed and Smaller Business*, Croner Publications, 1989

Maitland, Iain, *The Business Planner*, Butterworth–Heinemann, 1992

Mallory, Charles, *Direct Mail*, Kogan Page, 1992

Morris, M J, *Starting a Successful Small Business*, 2nd edn, Kogan Page, 1992

Pullen, Max, *Business Cash Books Made Easy*, Kogan Page, 1992

Rogers, Len, *Barclays Guide to Marketing*, Blackwell, 1990

Secrett, Malcolm, *Successful Budgeting in a Week*, Hodder & Stoughton, 1993

Treacy, Declan, *Successful Time Management in a Week*, Hodder & Stoughton, 1993

Video Arts, *So You Think You Can Cope With Customers?*, Mandarin/ Methuen, 1989

Williams, David, *Running Your Own Business*, Longman, 1990

Woodcock, Clive, *The Guardian Guide to Running a Small Business*, Kogan Page, 1988

Relevant acts and regulations

Cheques Act 1992
Consumer Protection Act 1987
Contracts of Employment 1972–1978

Data Protection Act 1984

EC Directives – Health and Safety 1993
Employment Act 1989
Equal Pay Act 1970

Fire Regulations Act 1976

Health and Safety at Work Act 1974

Misrepresentation Act 1967

Offices, Shops and Railway Premises Act 1963

Race Relations Act 1976
Reporting of Injuries, Diseases and Dangerous Occurrences
    Regulations 1985
Re-sale Prices Act 1964–1976

Sex Discrimination Act 1975
Supply of Goods and Services Act 1982

Trade Descriptions Act 1968
Trade Descriptions Act 1972

Associations

Association of Reflexologists
27 Old Gloucester Street
London WC1N 3XX

British Association of Beauty Therapy and Cosmetology
Mrs D Parkes
Parabola House
Parabola Road
Cheltenham
Gloucestershire GL50 3AH
Tel: 0242 570284

British Association of Electrolysists
18 Stokes End
Haddenham
Buckinghamshire HP17 8DX
Tel: 0844 290721

British Association of Skin Camouflage
Mrs Jane Goulding
25 Blackhorse Drive
Silkstone Common
Nr Barnsley
South Yorkshire S75 4SD
Tel: 0226 790744

Federation of Image Consultants
6 Victoria Street
St Albans
Hertfordshire AL1 3JB
Tel: 0272 44682

International Aestheticiennes
Bache Hall
Bache Hall Estate
Chester CH2 2BR
Tel: 0244 376539

International Federation of Aromatherapists
Department of Continuing Education
Royal Masonic Hospital
Ravenscourt Park
London W6 0TN
Tel: 081 846 8066

International Federation of Health and Beauty Therapists
38A Portsmouth Road
Woolston
Southampton
Hampshire SO2 9AD

International Mail Association (UK)
LSM House
2B Thornlaw Road
London SE27 0SA

Independent Professional Therapists International
8 Ordsall Road
Retford
Nottinghamshire DN22 7PL
Tel: 0777 700383

International Society of Professional Aromatherapists
Hinkley and District Hospital and Health Centre
The Annexe
Mount Road
Hinkley
Leicestershire LE10 1AE
Tel: 0455 637987

National Beauty Therapy Lecturers Association
Ms G Moore
18 Shotlery Grove
Walmley
Sutton Coldfield
West Midlands
B76 2QB
Tel: 021 351 3034

Awarding bodies

Business and Technology Education Council
Central House
Upper Woburn Place
London WC1H 0HH
Tel: 071 413 8400

City and Guilds London Institute
46 Britannia Street
London WC1 9RG
Tel: 071 278 2468

Confederation of International Beauty Therapy and Cosmetology
Mrs D Parkes
Parabola House
Parabola Road
Cheltenham
Gloucestershire
GL50 3AH
Tel: 0242 570284

International Aestheticiennes
Bache Hall
Bache Hall Estate
Chester CH2 2BR
Tel: 0244 376539

International Health and Beauty Council
109a Felpham Road
Felpham
West Sussex PO22 2PW
Tel: 0243 422695

International Therapy Examination Council
James House
Oakelbrook Hill
Newent
Gloucestershire GL18 1HD
Tel: 0531 821875

National Council for Vocational Qualifications
222 Euston Road
London NW1 2BZ
Tel: 071 387 9898

Scottish Vocational Education Council
Hanover House
24 Douglas Street
Glasgow G2 7NQ
Tel: 041 248 7900

Sources of information

Advisory Standards Authority
Brook House
2–16 Torrington Place
London WC1E 7HN

Advisory Conciliation and Arbitration
Service (ACAS) (Head Office)
Clifton House
83 Euston Road
London NW1 2RB
Tel: 071 388 5100

Association of British Chambers of Commerce
212 Shaftesbury Avenue
London WC2H 8EB

Association of British Insurers
Aldermary House
Queen Street
London EC4N 1TT

British Franchise Association
Franchise Chambers
Thames View
Newtown Road
Henley-on-Thames
Oxfordshire RG9 1HE
Tel: 0491 578050

British Insurance Brokers Association
BIBA House
14 Bevis Marks
London EC3A 7NT

Business in the Community
227a City Road
London EC1V 1LX

Companies Registration Office:
England and Wales
Companies House
Crown Way
Maindy
Cardiff CF4 3UZ

Northern Ireland
Dept of Economic Development
64 Chichester Street
Belfast BT1 4JX

Scotland
102 George Street
Edinburgh EH2 3DJ

Customs & Excise
New Kings Beam House
22 Upper Ground
London SE1 9PS

Data Protection Registrar
Springfield House
Water Lane
Wilmslow
Cheshire SK9 5AX
Tel: 0625 535711

Department of Employment
Caxton House
Tothill Street
London SW1H 9NF
Tel: 071 273 3000

Department of Social Security (DSS)
(Refer to your telephone directory for
the nearest office.)

Department of the Environment (DOE)
2 Marsham Street
London SW1P 3EB
Tel: 071 276 3000

England and Wales; see Scottish Division or DOE Scotland

Department of the Environment (DOE) (Northern Ireland)
Town and Country Planning Service
Commonwealth House
35 Castle Street
Belfast TR1 1GU
Tel: 0232 321212

Environmental health officers are employed by local authorities –
telephone numbers will be in 'Business and Services Directory'
or 'Thomson Local Directory'.

Equal Opportunities Commission
Overseas House
Quay Street
Manchester M3 3HN
Tel: 061 833 9244

Federation of Microsystems Centres
3 Heaton Road
Newcastle-upon-Tyne NE6 1SA
Tel: 091 276 6288

Health and Safety Executive Head Office
Baynards House
1 Chepstow Place
Westbourne Grove
London W2 4TF
Tel: 071 221 0870

Health and Safety Executive (HSE)
St Hugh's House
Stanley Precinct
Bootle
Merseyside L20 3QY
Tel: 051 951 4000

In Business Now
Freepost
London SW1E 5YZ

National Federation of Self-Employed and Small Businesses
32 St Annes Road West
Lytham St Annes
Lancashire FY8 1NY

Office of Fair Trading
Consumer Credit Licensing Branch
Government Building
Bromyard Avenue
London W3 7BB
Tel: 081 242 2858

Scottish Business in the Community
Eagle Star House
25 St Andrews Square
Edinburgh EH2 1AF

Scottish Development Agency
120 Bothwell Street
Glasgow G2 7JP

Scottish Industry Department (IDS)
Sandyford Road
Paisley
Glasgow G2 6AT

Small Firms Division DTI
Steel House
Tothill Street
London SW1H 9NF

RECRUITMENT

Health & Beauty Recruitment Ltd
28 Bolton Street
Mayfair
London W1Y 8HB
Tel: 071 491 9771/2

ADVERTISING

Thomas Directories
Thomson House
296 Farnborough Road
Farnborough
Hampshire GU14 7NU
Tel: 0252 516111

MAGAZINES

Hairdressers' Journal Health & Beauty Salon
Quadrant House
The Quadrant
Sutton
Surrey SM2 5AS
Tel: 081 661 3500

International Journal of Aromatherapy
PO Box 746
Hove
East Sussex BN3 3XA
Tel: 0273 772479

Les Nouvelles Esthetiques
Exhibition House
Spring Street
London W2 3RB
Tel: 071 262 2886

Suppliers

Equipment and products

Carlton Professional
Taylor Reeson
Commerce Way
Lancing
Sussex BN15 8TA
Tel: 0903 761100
Fax: 0903 751111

Depilex
2 Marsh Lane
Nantwich
Cheshire CW5 5HH
Tel: 0270 628091
Fax: 0270 629681

Ellisons
Crondal Road
Exhall
Coventry CV7 9NH
Tel: 0203 361619
Fax: 0203 644010

HOF House of Famuir
The Grange
Beeston Green
Sandy
Bedfordshire SG19 1PG
Tel: 0767 682288
Fax: 0767 682266

George Solly Organisation Ltd
111 Watlington Street
Reading
Berkshire RG1 4RQ
Tel: 0734 566477
Fax: 0734 566318

Products

House of Neroli
Aromatherapy Products
Oakelbrook Mill
Newent, Gloucestershire
Tel: 0531 821875
Fax: 0531 822425

Medex
Medex House
53–53A Belswains Lane
Hemel Hempstead
Hertfordshire HP3 9PP
Tel: 0442 249797

Susan Molyneux
9 King Street
Cheltenham
Gloucestershire
Tel: 0242 570515

Salon wear

Aston & Fincher Ltd
8 Holyhead Road
Birmingham B21 0LY
Tel: 021 523 9340
Fax: 021 554 5897

Florence Ruby
Caddick Road
Knowsley Industrial Park South
Merseyside L34 9HP
Tel: 051 548 2228
Fax: 051 549 2011

Index